Rocio,

Live Life

Engaged!

Dario,

Live Life
Engineer!

ENGAGED MANAGEMENT

VOLUME 3

AWAKENING SALES CONFIDENCE IN YOUR TEAM

JOHN HANNON

ENGAGED MANAGEMENT
VOLUME 3
AWAKENING SALES CONFIDENCE IN YOUR TEAM

John Hannon Media, LLC
7762 Silver Bell Drive
Sarasota, FL 34241

(937) 776-4997
john@johnhannonmedia.com
www.johnhannonmedia.com

Also by John Hannon

ENGAGED MANAGEMENT
VOLUME 1
INSPIRING YOUR TEAM TO WIN

AND

ENGAGED MANAGEMENT
VOLUME 2
MAXIMIZING YOUR TEAM'S SALES
PERFORMANCE

Available at:

www.amazon.com
www.johnhannonmedia.com

CONTENTS

CHAPTER 2
COACHING TO WIN

CHAPTER 3
MANAGING FOR MAXIMUM PERFORMANCE

CHAPTER 4
SALES PREPARATION AND PLANNING

CHAPTER 5
WITHOUT CUSTOMERS YOU HAVE NO BUSINESS

CHAPTER 6
FOCUS ON YOUR CAREER

THE FINAL LESSON

ABOUT THE AUTHOR

ACKNOWLEDGEMENTS

To all my clients, family and friends, it is only because of your dedicated support and encouragement that I have enjoyed career success. Many of you believed in me when I didn't believe in myself. To you, I will be forever indebted and grateful.

John Hannon
Sarasota, Florida
September 2019

FOREWORD

You are about to read a book on Engaged Management. I suspect you want to improve your personal management skills. And, whether you manage a staff of thousands or maybe just a few, you want to be as effective a leader as possible. Now, think of your team—the various characters and personalities who execute your vision. What would they say about your management skills today? What do you want them to say about your management skills tomorrow? Would your veteran staff call you a "leader," who treats them with respect and allows them to exercise their talents? What about your newest hire? Would they say you inspire them and are committed to their growth in your company? Does the thought of reading the comments of someone you manage scare you, even just a little?

If you're John Hannon, the answers don't scare you. I know this because I've worked for John for years, and he asked me to write this foreword.

I've learned so many lessons from John over the years; lessons like we treat our stars differently, always make deposits, and numbers don't lie. I've admired his eagle-eye attention to detail, his systems of accountability, and his careful planning and radical consistency of our brand. And the good news is, John shares all of his wisdom in this book. John's three-book *Engaged Management* series is best-selling because he truly is the authority on engaging individuals, reinforcing their importance to the organization, and creating cultures that generate continuous positive momentum. I have witnessed all of this firsthand. It was under John's guidance that I authored my first book, a feat that might not have been accomplished if it weren't for John constantly asking, "So Tom, when is your book going to be done?" It was also through his determination that both John and I earned the designation of Certified Speaking Professional (CSP), the highest earned accreditation of the National Speakers Association that includes just over 1% of the 53,000+ speakers worldwide. It was important to John that we earn our CSP recognition together, adding extra meaning to the accomplishment. For years, I've watched John uplift our staff, grow people to levels they never thought they'd achieve, and make very tough decisions when they were needed.

So, congratulations on taking the initiative to improve your management skillset. Your purchase and study of this book is evidence that you are in the very top percentage of managers across the country. The next step to improving your colleague, employee, vendor, client, and even family connections is to take action on the incredible wealth of knowledge that John has laboriously packed into these pages.

Engaged Management: Volume 3, Awakening Sales Confidence In Your Team is best consumed with a highlighter, a notepad, and an open mind. This "can't put down" book is one that you will want to mark up and dogear for post-read referencing. This resource deserves priority placement among your favorite business and self-help books, as it will provide an infinite return on your investment. You will experience enlightenment, clarity, and quick success as you begin to incorporate the strategies and guidance into your day-to-day operations, from the topic's expert and thought leader, John Hannon.

So, put down your device, pick up this book, dig in, discover, and deploy.

Tom Ray (tom@jimdoyle.com) is the Executive Vice President of Jim Doyle & Associates. He is a Certified Speaking Professional and one of the most popular and requested keynote speakers in the media and marketing industries. Tom's book, *Branding is OUT, Results are IN! Lessons for the LOCAL Advertiser* was an Amazon best-seller.

INTRODUCTION

You are holding in your hands, the third and final book of the *Engaged Management* trilogy. The dream for this series started nearly six years ago. A lot has changed since then.

Now, consolidation of business is the norm, as a "bigger for leverage" mentality crosses all industries. Pressure from bean counters to achieve a number for the street has removed some of the passion, or the reason, most of us got into media in the first place. Many employees feel underappreciated, as their names have been replaced with numbers and their roles have evolved into double and triple the responsibility, resulting in ever-expanding workweek hours for the same, or even less, compensation.

Yes, our business has changed.

As our business has changed, so too have management styles. In response to increased pressures, some managers have buried themselves deeper behind closed doors, with little time for subordinates. Long days are filled with creating

1

spreadsheets and justifying shortfalls in preparation for performance questions from corporate.

Other managers respond to the increasing pressures by telling, demanding or even threatening, their voice escalating in tone and volume. Team members lose confidence and fear they'll be the next one singled out. They begin to question why they should continue to stay in a negative environment.

The best managers are leaders. They position themselves as a buffer between company demands and staff momentum. They recognize that during times of change the most important question employees have, but often don't ask, is, "How does this affect me?"

These leaders clarify how individual performance affects and contributes to the big picture. They create cultures that are professionally accountable, high-performing, and believe in celebrating wins. They praise publicly and correct privately. They understand their team members' goals and ambitions. They sacrifice. They care about family. They lead by example.

These leaders recognize that their effort is better spent side-by-side in the trenches, motivating individuals, instead of spending hours building a defense of spreadsheets. Over time, word gets out and they have no problem finding good people because good people flock to positive cultures.

These leaders are the minority in any industry. However, they are easily recognized. Simply look for the individuals who carry themselves confidently and possess a self-assured smile when all others have a look of uncertainty. They build special connections by dropping the task at hand to give their full attention to the concern. They recognize that the strength derived from the support of the team is infinitely stronger than anything they could accomplish on their own.

Long after their departures, these stars are spoken of fondly and are the bright spots of many careers. They have discovered the secret to career connection through *Engaged Management*.

CHAPTER 1

LEADING THE TEAM

A boss has the title, a leader has the people.

-Simon Sinek

HELLO FROM LAS VEGAS

Every April, I leave the National Association of Broadcasters convention in Las Vegas a bit lighter in the wallet but heavier with knowledge. Being an early adopter tech geek, it's a lot of fun for me to learn about recent technology breakthroughs like 4k UHDTV, 8k Super Hi-Vision, ATSC 3.0, and miniature drone advancements.

But that's not the purpose of my trip. In fact, most years the convention floor eludes me. Instead, the days are filled with conversations wherever there's an available chair to catch up with current and prospective clients and industry friends. Inevitably, a few themes or concerns will bubble up from these meetings providing great insight as to the topics that are keeping the TV group C-suites awake at night.

Many years, the usual concerns of sales metrics and sustained post-political performance kick off a lot of discussions. After all, we're in the revenue business. However, this particular year, there was another topic expressed in quiet whispers—futures—specifically, the impact of the spectrum auction (and what will the real valuations bring) and speculation on who's acquiring properties and who may sell. Given the no-one-could-have-guessed transactions that have taken place in our industry over the last few years, it was unlikely that any short-term ownership change of hands would be a surprise.

As industry players speculate, so does the industry press. Chances are, a great number of your employees read this press, where the mere mention of your employer's name can send dedicated employees into a "what if" frenzy. Supposed "in the know" individuals stir the pot at the water cooler, and soon, you have a staff concerned about trying to piece together buy and sale scenarios, which results in a loss of focus on the media outlet's sales and operational priorities at hand.

The best way to minimize staff concern is to gather the team to make a statement and to be available to field answers on the topic as soon as possible. Honesty is definitely the best policy in this scenario, but it should also be common sense that there will likely be information that you simply cannot release to the team.

So, what do you tell the staff?

Encourage them to do their absolute best work. There is no better moment to shine than when a company is in transition. The most valuable assets to any company are competent and high-performing personnel. If your sellers are identified as such, whether the company is being bought or sold, they will likely prosper through the change.

What about managers? To you, and your leadership team, I would say the same thing. Now is the moment for your absolute best work. There was a time when the acquiring company held all the cards and populated their new acquisitions with their own talent. However, today's companies are getting so big that they don't have enough of their own managers to transition to the new properties. This situation creates opportunity for managers of the acquired outlets.

It's an exciting time for our business. And, unlike the roulette wheel losses I experienced this trip in Las Vegas, the return of TV industry mergers and acquisitions to our industry headlines is a safe bet.

IT'S TIME FOR A SALES MEETING WITHOUT A MANAGER

Often, new sales managers want so desperately to prove themselves worthy of their new title that they have trouble saying "no." They eagerly welcome delegation from their superiors and are as equally eager to accept jobs from AE's who delegate tasks up. Long term, the eagerness turns to resentment because the manager is spending so much time working "in" the business that he or she has little time to work "on" the business. It's a never-ending treadmill, causing the manager to wish for more hours in the day or daydream of the good times on the street, when they were helping clients exceed their marketing goals.

This topic came up in a conversation with a less-than-six-months-minted sales manager, who was not only burning the candle at both ends, but also feeling underappreciated by a sales team that had grown a bit apathetic to the importance of making budget. His team had missed the total revenue target the last four consecutive months.

My suggestion was to have his staff host a sales meeting without him present. You can imagine his look of confusion in response to my suggestion.

It was apparent to me that the sales team lacked "skin" in the game and the sales manager was carrying an almost unbearable load. It was time to shift some of that load back to the team.

I asked the manager to pick two mature leaders– ones he could trust and who had the respect of their sales peers. Next, he should express to the sales leaders his concern(s) over the team's lack of drive, which is directly related to the team's lackluster revenue performance, and ask them to host a sales meeting, without any sales managers present. The goal of the meeting would be for the team to walk away with very specific expectations for each individual on the staff. Each category—for example, number of calls, new business volume, special projects, digital revenue, existing client increases, etc.—should have a very specific time and number bound to expectations for every individual on the team. Each goal should be attainable, and when combined, should exceed the revenue needed to get the team over the budget number.

The team leaders are then responsible for covering the plan with the sales manager. The role of the sales manager in this exercise is to ensure the goals are realistic, so the plan isn't doomed from the start. In an effort to please, teams given this opportunity may sometimes be too aggressive with their goals. Believe it or not, a manager may need to correct a daily call goal of something like 12 appointments a day down to something more manageable, like 5.

Many positives come out of this exercise. First, since they created the plan, the sales team tends to be more enthusiastic in their effort. In reality, they have unknowingly created accountability for themselves. Second, a manager is able to build a bench of potential future managers, based upon their acceptance and fulfillment of the delegated responsibilities. Lastly, a sales manager frees up much needed time and, through delegation, builds cheerleaders who are, in effect, unpaid sales management assistants, encouraging the team to execute by the plan.

A CULTURE CHANGE REQUIRES BUY-IN

Many managers spend countless hours mapping a culture change, only to run out of gas and give up on the process prematurely.

In this scenario, when a manager "gives up," it's most likely because they're a single individual trying to force change on an entire department that lacks buy-in. Disappointment arrives quickly, as the expected progress isn't made, and the anticipated positive culture change begins to spin deeper into negativity. The unsuccessful manager may become bitter and telegraph their disappointment to the rest of the team. Her/his actions do nothing more than pile undesirable traits onto an already questionable culture.

So, how does one get "buy-in" to create a ground swell that becomes the key to pushing through a change, and ultimately, positively impacting culture?

The first step is to help others understand what their buy-in gets them. In other words, what's in it for them.

My first sales manager in the television business

was Dale Woods. He was never shy about sharing his new-found knowledge—gained from stacks of self-help, sales, and business books—with the team. It wasn't long before his career flourished, and he was rewarded with multiple general manager posts. In fact, he was *Broadcasting & Cable* magazine's 2012 General Manager of the Year.

When Dale was a new sales manager, he installed a few rules, in an effort to change the office culture. The first of those rules was that meetings would start on time, and absolutely no one was allowed to be late. Dale even boasted that if *he* could make it to the meetings on time, every time, then so could everyone else. Did I mention that Dale lived 45 minutes from the station, yet his car was the first in the parking lot every morning?

For the first month or so, most improved their arrival times, and there were very few late attendees to meetings. However, a *few* late was not the goal. *No one ever* late was the goal. So, Dale announced another rule, "From this day forward, any individual who's late for our meeting is responsible for bringing doughnuts for the entire team to the next meeting." An AE chimed in, "Yeah, and they have to be FRESH doughnuts, not those day-old, stale leftovers." The entire room broke out in a cheer of approval, and suddenly, Dale's effort to get everyone to the meeting on time became the team's effort. There was buy-in because each individual's win was a fresh doughnut. Dale never had to police late arrivals again. That job was taken by AE's who were now the official, self-designated, timekeepers. They passed judgement on who was on time, who was late, and who was responsible for paying the "fine" of fresh doughnuts at the next meeting.

Because Dale's car was always the first in the parking lot, it was time for celebration when, on one meeting day, employees pulling up to the station noticed Dale's car wasn't there. The word in the hallway was, "Yes! He's finally going to be late and will have to buy *us* doughnuts!"

Imagine the look on the team's face when Dale strolled into the conference room 2 minutes before the meeting was to start.

Apparently, his car had thrown a crank shaft pulley and he was stranded on I-75. His first thought was not about his car and what to do with it, but rather, "There's no way in heck I'm going to be late to our meeting!" So, he left his car on the interstate and hitched a ride from a passerby to the office. When he retells the story, he lights up, reminded of everyone's look of shock when he walked into the meeting, even though his car wasn't in the parking lot.

That kind of management commitment deletes nearly every previously acceptable excuse for being late to a meeting.

Managers who go to the extreme example are held in high esteem by their teams. Or, maybe the staff thinks the manager is a bit obsessed, or nuts!

THE QUICK EXECUTION OF KNOWLEDGE IS POWER

As I was writing this, I was still coming down from the euphoria of sharing, interacting, listening, and networking at the Jim Doyle & Associates biennial Sales Manager's High Performance Boot Camp.

Imagine, if you will, spending almost three days with nearly 200 of some of the smartest and most optimistic management minds in the broadcasting business. Add to that opportunity, incredible presentations from *four* Hall Of Fame speakers. Kick in a healthy dose of laughs and some pretty good food in sunny Tampa, Florida, far away from the January snow and cold in the rest of the country. The result is an incredibly productive event, where ideas are shared, challenged, and captured. The event becomes an opportunity to recharge career batteries, reset business practices, and revamp cultures.

To those who have ever attended a JDA Boot Camp, I want to congratulate you for taking the initiative to "better" yourself. The fact that you sacrificed a weekend to attend this event speaks volumes about your dedication.

You may have previously heard the quote, "Knowledge is power." There was a day, in our world of television, when that quote may have held some legitimacy. But today, our industry continues a cycle of tremendous change, and the challenges presented to managers and leaders are almost overwhelming.

Rupert Murdoch stated, *"The world is changing very fast. Big will not beat small anymore; it will be the fast beating the slow."* With that in mind, it would stand to reason that knowledge is *not* power. The *quick execution* of knowledge is power.

The star television managers who convened in Tampa understand that concept and are sure to benefit in many ways from the experience.

In a phone call shortly after Boot Camp, one of those managers asked me if I was tired. Admittedly, I was *physically* tired. Three days of little sleep, platform speaking, and running microphones around a ballroom can have that effect on a body. However, thanks to multiple hours of interaction with managers eagerly seeking new levels of performance, my *mental energy* was at its peak, so much so that I had trouble sleeping in anticipation of getting to the office to put my own new-found knowledge to work!

WHAT IS YOUR MINIMUM MONTHLY DOLLAR AMOUNT?

What is the minimum monthly dollar amount an advertiser would have to invest in the power of your TV station(s) or outlet and digital products in order to be successful?

It's amazing to me the number of managers who don't know the answer to that question.

The importance of understanding this "minimum" sets the expectations for your team of sellers. If you have determined that the minimum monthly investment to be successful is, for example, $6,500, then we can assume that any number below that mark will likely end in disappointing results for the client.

Over time, if your sellers close business below the $6,500 monthly, client campaigns become less than effective and your AE's will begin to suspect that your TV programming and digital options don't work. Naturally, if a seller doesn't believe in what they're selling, it doesn't get sold. Having as few as *two* superstar AE's on your staff with this attitude can dramatically alter the positive momentum of your team, creating a month after month missed-budget spiral. Soon, the whole team begins selling out of fear and desperation, trying to close business inside the month and effectively running on a treadmill of catch-up.

Is that a dramatic description? Maybe... or maybe not... when one considers that the whole scenario can be avoided if a manager clearly reinforces the minimum monthly investment expectation to the sales team. Doing so provides a benchmark for sellers and a professional "I told you so" opportunity to reel in the naysayers.

Having been in your shoes, I recognize that there are times when it is necessary to close an agreement that may be *just short* of the stated monthly minimum. In those instances, it's imperative that your AE's have a client conversation at the front-end of the process to set expectations. For example,

"Mrs. Prospect, unless you can allocate more dollars, your budget is just short of what we deem to be the acceptable monthly minimum in order for you to maximize marketing success with our company. However, I'm willing to help make your dollars work with a few select programs and some very targeted digital geofencing. But, as you begin to experience success resulting from your exposure to our audience, I would ask that you be open to a conversation maybe 30, 60 or 90 days later to discuss stepping up to the monthly minimum, or a greater investment, to allow you to enjoy an even larger return on your investment. Make sense?"

By setting this expectation, the clients understand that upon collecting their new-found profits resulting from targeting your audience, they'll need to increase their investment with you before, or even if, they consider spending with your competitors.

WOULD YOU LIKE FRIES WITH THAT?

It was nearing the end of 1999, when I, as station manager, sat across the table from group owner,

16

Dan Sullivan, sweating out the annual budget discussion. As we closed our numbers-filled binders, Dan delivered one more question, "John, will you get the station to that number next year?" My response was simply, "Dan, I'll die trying!"

Dan asked the question again, but changed his tone just enough to convey that there are only two answers to the question—yes or no.

I immediately answered, "Yes," and Dan responded, "Good, because if not, you'll be saying, 'Would you like fries with that?'"

As a kid, did you ever hear the rhyme, *sticks and stones may break my bones, but words can never harm me?*" In just 13 words, Dan Sullivan was able to prove that popular children's rhyme wrong, and it scared me to death!

While doing a bit of recruiting research, that memory resurfaced when I stumbled on a story in *USA Today*. The edition was dated January 25, 2018. The headline read: In-N-Out Managers Make $160,000 Per Year.

No, that's not a misprint. You read it right—$160,000 per year!

In-N-Out Burger VP of Operations, Denny Warnick, explained that company founders, Harry and Esther Snyder, believed, "Quality service requires quality employees with quality pay... and paying their associates well was just one way to help maintain focus."

Never in my wildest dreams did the occupation of flipping burgers surface as a six-figure salary position. However, according to the report, In-N-Out workers start at around $13 an hour and can work their way up to managing a single, fast-food chain location, making an average of $160,000—without a college education!

This appears to be the front end of industries paying eye-popping dollars to retain the right talent. As you have likely experienced in today's business environment, not just *good*, but *great*, talent is hard to find, recruit, and maintain. The most talented individuals are commanding money—big money—and companies are finding that by digging a bit deeper into their wallets, they're able to speak to, and provide, careers for the top tier of performers in their industries.

So, how does news like this affect our business of media sales?

As of this writing, there's no research to indicate salaries are dropping in the media industry. However, one could easily assume such if they overheard my travel discussions with high-level managers. And, if our incomes are going down while other businesses are increasing their offers, couldn't we safely assume that we stand to lose some of our best talent to businesses outside of our own?

It wasn't uncommon for television and

broadcasting sales and station managers to reach out to the Jim Doyle & Associates headquarters to confidentially discuss individuals they would like to recruit, or even opportunities that they, themselves, were considering. Often, the "money topic" would quickly become a major part of our discussion. Comments like, "My company won't let me offer any more money for this position," or "I never made that kind of money when I was 'X' manager," were fairly common.

The biggest confusion comes from top-performing sellers who have been tapped to get their first management stripe via a local sales manager role. For a number of years, it has been an acceptable practice to offer a new LSM a package that pays less than they made as an account executive. I never understood that practice. The LSM has to be equally capable of selling inside, as well as outside, the station(s). They become a dumping ground for all the necessary "dirty" work and conversations, and the job certainly comes with an extra helping of stress. Yet, their perceived value is established with statements like, "In the first year, if you drive the staff to deliver all this extra revenue, you'll hit all your bonuses and make just $15K less than you did last year. Keep up the budget-making leadership, and we should be able to get you whole in your second year as LSM." That kind of thinking is why good folks are leaving us.

If you don't want to lose your ability to recruit a local sales management star and are truly in a situation where your company simply will not step up to the dollars you need, consider adding performance incentives to the offer.

For example, let's say your offer is $30K short of bringing in someone who could be an incredible LSM to guide your local sales team. Don't let the shortfall stop you from sweetening the offer. If you typically pay AE's 15% commission on local business, then $30K is only $200K in local billing. You can then say to the prospective LSM, "If you prospect and close $200K in local billing your first year, I'll add an additional $30K on top of my current offer." It's commission you'd have had to pay an AE anyway, so the dollars aren't associated with "additional" expenses.

Utilizing this kind of performance incentive provides more than the obvious LSM/station win-win. The additional $200K goes to the new business revenue line since these are "prospected," not existing, dollars. The action of closing new accounts creates sales credibility and respect for the new LSM among the sales team. Lastly, the $200K from year one can be used as foundational money for a new AE hire in year two or for incentives in the absence of a new AE hire.

There are certainly other ways to get to an acceptable dollar offer. The "how" varies with each company. Make sure to explore the variables and get credit for this kind of out-of-the-box thinking by working in tandem and exchanging thoughts on this topic with your superiors. Otherwise, the incredible management talent you had hoped to add to your sales team will consider a career change, maybe even embracing the question, "Would you like fries with that?"

A MIRROR IS THE GREATEST ACCOUNTABILITY TOOL

A mirror is often described as the greatest accountability tool. It provides a perfect reflection of positive and negative feedback to the only individual who can change current circumstances.

Sometimes, the mirror is capable of surprising with unsolicited feedback. I was reminded of this thought at a high school weightlifting meet.

My oldest daughter, Madison, carried a list of goals that she wanted to accomplish to end her high school experience on a high note. One of her top goals was to qualify for the Florida High School Girls Weightlifting State Championships.

Madison was capable of lifting much more than her body weight of 139 pounds. In fact, as she continued her quest to the state championships, she finished in the top three of her weight class at every meet leading up to the championships.

At one of these meets, Madison easily completed a lift securing first place. As she came off the platform, I gave her a too-quick congratulations and then proceeded to explain how she should have attempted more weight because the lift was too easy for her. In mid-sentence of expanding on this thought, in a mirror adjacent to the weight racks, I saw the real-time reflection of the scowl on my face. The non-verbals were confrontational, complete with finger pointing. I was raining down negativity on my daughter over her first-place finish! Ugh. Immediately, realizing this mistake, I pulled Madison in for a long hug of apology, congratulations, and love.

In my television market visits, it was not uncommon for the lack of appreciation topic to surface in conversations with both sellers and managers. It seems in today's rush for the dollar, sometimes the importance of positive engagement with employees is minimized. Often, a congratulations gets lost as it's grouped in with a negative, or, worse yet, the positive is never expressed.

Did you ever hear of the manager who responded, "It's about time," or "Great, what else did you sell?" to an account executive who was expressing their excitement over a new business contract they just closed? Or, maybe you've met the manager who told the AE, "Nice job on making budget this month, but you fell short on your sports sales." How many seconds were spent basking in the glory of making budget in that communication—one and a half?!

Think how defeating those comments are to the seller. Just one statement has the ability to railroad any positive momentum that could result from the victory of a sale or performance.

A true expression of your appreciation, congratulations, and excitement for whatever the victory is will go a long way in your relationships. Focus on the celebration of the moment and save the judgment for another conversation.

THE POWER OF POSITIVE COMMENTS

On this particular day, I went to the grocery store for a "staples" trip. It was one of those days when I wasn't really paying attention to anyone—didn't really want to talk to anyone—I just wanted to get the groceries and go home.

The lady at the meat counter changed my attitude. She greeted me with a smile and asked how she could be of service. She sliced the first cut of turkey, came back to the counter showing me the cut, and asked if it was the right thickness. Then she proceeded to hand me the slice of lunch meat to enjoy while she completed my order (wow, there's a customer service tip for other grocery stores.)

But it was really at the end of the transaction when my attitude took a turn for the better as the worker offered a sincere smile and said, "Enjoy the rest of your day." The message was conveyed in such a way that I didn't just hear the words, I felt them. The wish resonated so much that I caught myself smiling while walking to the checkout and decided to pass my smile along to someone else.

Stepping into the cash register lane, I complimented the lady in front of me on the lovely color of her blouse. She responded, "Thank you so much. You know, my granddaughter doesn't like this thing. I'll have to tell her someone else agrees with me!"

The next positive deposit victim was the bagger. When he asked if he could carry the bags to my car, I replied that he was working entirely too hard in the hot weather. He should stay inside in the air conditioning. He thanked me profusely and still had a smile on his face when I exited the store.

Years ago, when in your chair, I used to walk the office, consciously on the lookout for sincere deposits to employees. The comments generally centered on whatever hit me at the time—the color of a tie, new glasses or shiny shoes, or maybe extra work like shoveling snow in the entry. Any topic that created smiles and showed appreciation was game.

Selfishly, offering these comments always provided a lift for me. It's fun to make people feel good. But the bonus is, when done sincerely, these comments provide a lift to the receiver that, just like my encounter at the grocery store, tends to be shared. This positive momentum is key in establishing environments and cultures where people *want* to work.

Once, a manager asked me, "What can I do to let an employee know how much I appreciate them?"

My response? "When you're at a loss as to what to say to a star and complimenting them on the color of their tie doesn't seem like enough, simply tell them what's in your heart. Try something like, "Hey, Sheryl. I was just thinking of your work a few days ago and wanted to tell you how much you're appreciated around here. We're only as good as we are because of your dedication, hard work, and effort. So, thank you, thank you, thank you."

Then, as you're feeling good about making someone else feel good, get out of the way and let Sheryl deliver her smile to her coworkers!

A MISSED OPPORTUNITY

A member of our leadership team returned from a road trip with a disappointing story. Apparently, a high-performing account executive (fictitiously named "Karen") was frustrated after a TV station visit from her older sister. The sister served as Karen's mentor and work "sounding board" and this was her first visit to the TV station.

Karen excitedly welcomed her sister at the

reception area and commenced a behind-the-scenes tour of the TV facility. After stops at the news set and pleasant interactions with the on-air talent, the pair made their way to the sales offices. The first stop was to meet the General Sales Manager, who said, "Nice to meet you... and Karen, what the heck were you thinking with these low rates? Now we have a backlog of pre-empts!"

The conversation with the Local Sales Manager wasn't much better, as he turned to Karen's sister and stated, "It is a pleasure meeting you. The bulk of my job is spent keeping Karen from going off the deep end."

"That's not exactly how I had hoped to impress my big sister," Karen explained.

Karen is an absolute star, a sales team leader, a staff work horse, and her clients are raving fans. She proudly wears her station colors and brags to her family about her chosen career, office, and co-workers. Yet, her managers were so consumed with the day-to-day that they missed the opportunity to make an incredible deposit with one of their best employees. The biggest issue is that unless they're reading this, these managers have probably never given their conversation with Karen and her sister a second thought. They likely have no clue how their words hurt Karen.

The best leaders are always on the lookout for opportunities to honor their stars. In Karen's situation, the managers should have loudly proclaimed what a valuable asset, leader, and star she is, and how the office would somehow be "less than" were she not on the team. Karen would have beamed, her loyalty to the station managers would have been cemented, and her sister would have been impressed.

The next time you find yourself greeting a team member's guest, embrace the moment as an opportunity for a positive deposit. Your star employee will be glad that you did!

GETTING A GENERAL SALES MANAGER RETURN ON INVESTMENT

If you're a General Manager or higher inside a media organization, I do hope you'll take seriously the information I'm about to reveal to you.

Recently, I was on the receiving end of a message from a veteran General Sales Manager who was questioning her lack of enthusiasm for her role. With a self-defeating tone she stated, "I do not like the job of GSM anymore. I don't get out of the office; I'm a report-maker. And, the expectations of our company to sell projects is turning our team into peddlers, which goes against everything I know and love about this business. I sometimes want to just take a list, give up the stress of management, and hit the streets again. What I used to love about this business is getting in front of clients and really digging in with my sellers. There's no time for that anymore. GSM's today are chess masters. We move the pieces around, staff-up, and then report to a half dozen people or more at any given time, churning reports on what and why we didn't sell, and what we are going to sell."

Wow! Please do me a favor and carefully re-read the General Sales Manager's comments. How do you feel after digesting her words?

The sad thing is that this GSM is an incredible leader and is known for blowing the doors off budgets. But that was yesterday. Today, this manager is struggling with trying to balance the time demands of satisfying and selling her multiple bosses inside the company against motivating, mentoring, and teaching her account executives. Arguably, the best setting for sales training with AEs—a client meeting—has become the exception for this manager, not the rule.

Did you feel sympathy for the general sales manager after reading her comments or did you conclude that she's burned out and would be better served stepping back to a non-management seller's role?

The reality is, when she was accompanying her team on four-legged client calls—by her count, as many as 10-12 appointments a week—the closing ratio and new business dollars were greater and churn was minimized. An unanticipated positive was the boost to morale, as she was able to spend one-on-one time to give attention to, and engage with, each individual seller.

In which capacity can this manager better serve a television sales organization: 1) a client visible, lead-by-example AE mentor; or 2) a glorified paper-pusher with a big sales management title? OK, admittedly, I loaded the answers with descriptions to make #1 obvious. But, don't you think you pay entirely too much for the services of a GSM to have them spending the majority of their time on non-sales priorities; on things that aren't moving the sales team to surpass those large year-over-year revenue goals?

It's time for you to get your return on investment (ROI) from your General Sales Manager. Your role is to remove as many roadblocks as possible; anything that you can identify as superfluous time-wasters that can be revised, delegated or pulled entirely from your GSM's day-to day. That will free up the necessary time for dedication to selling priorities, in turn, maximizing your GSM ROI.

Finally, I understand that roles are different given market sizes, situations, and circumstances. In fact, in some television offices, GSM's may act as quasi-assistant General Managers. However, that does not relieve them of the duty to hit the streets with AE's. In fact, in the best performing stations, every manager from General Manager,

General Sales Manager, Local Sales Manager, Digital Sales Manager, and Creative Services Manager has a minimum monthly expectation of four-legged AE client calls. In one station, even the National Sales Manager is required to go on at least five local AE client calls a month. Doing so increases the station's local visibility, establishes credibility between AE's and the NSM, and helps build a management bench, preparing the NSM for the opportunity to be promoted to GSM, without having held the title of LSM.

ABOVE THE LINE VS. BELOW THE LINE THINKING

It was late in the day and I was driving back to the airport to catch another red-eye. While flipping through the radio dial, I stumbled upon the tail end of a business interview.

The discussion centered on the ability of great managers to motivate their teams through constructive communication. These managers quickly think about the outcome they desire and respond accordingly. Generally, their responses allow them to stay positive and rise above the circumstances. This is called "above the line" thinking.

Conversely, "below the line" thinking is a knee jerk or automated response to uncomfortable situations. More often than not, the response is negative and defensive. This kind of thinking can slow forward progress and may sometimes turn smaller problems into larger ones. While listening to the interview, I was reminded of a meeting I had once requested of my supervisor years ago. The intent was to have a delicate conversation about some friction I was sensing in our relationship that I suspected she was also feeling. It was important to "put the cards" on the table, as we were about to embark on a major task, and any misunderstandings in our relationship could have the potential to sideline our progress.

Careful thought went into planning the tone of the meeting. It was an out-of-the-office lunch in a quiet corner of a casual restaurant. I had prepared a *ten*-slide PowerPoint with plenty of pauses for explanation and discussion. My tone was going to be non-accusatory and absolutely respectful. After no less than a half-dozen practice run-throughs, I felt confident that together my manager and I could make some headway, professionally attacking the elephant on the table. I was determined to approach this meeting with nothing short of above the line thinking.

The lunch started pleasantly enough, at least until I pulled out the laptop. At that point, our smiles were semi-forced as we approached what we both knew could be a difficult conversation.

As the slides passed, so did the pleasantries. In

fact, when the presentation ended, our quiet corner picked up volume when my manager, while furiously pointing at the laptop, loudly exclaimed, "I know one thing is for absolute certain, there is no way in #@&^> that is going to happen!"

From time to time, my manager could raise her voice, but, in general, she wasn't a daily yeller and screamer. Her response and conversation post-presentation was the complete opposite of how I envisioned the meeting would end. Her immediate surface-level frustration was served up without thought to the outcome. It was below the line thinking.

Weeks later, as my wife, Bridget, and I drove by "the restaurant," I joked that I suffer from PTSD as a result of the lunch that took place there.

Both my manager and I lost a bit of trust for each other at that meeting. For quite a while after the lunch, I found myself less than enthusiastic to engage her and was always careful with our communication, not wanting to set her off again.

One never knows the potential impact of words and tone. Together, they have the ability to provide motivation or discouragement.

The next time you find yourself in a decision-making situation that demands a response, employ above the line thinking and take a split-second to consider the outcome of your words.

I BROKE MY LEG AND OUR CLIENTS BARELY NOTICED

It was just before lunch on my 51st birthday, when I decided to scale a ladder to test the fit of a door. It was time to see if my attempt to camouflage the 8-foot-high storage cubby in our master bedroom was successful.

Now, as I recall the helpless fall backward, grabbing at the air for anything to right my balance, it feels almost surreal. I knew upon landing that something was broken, but still, it was surprising to learn that surgery would be required to place screws and 2 plates to bring together the 4 bone breaks in and around my tibia leg bone.

The fall happened 48 hours before I was to board a plane to Atlanta for a 2-day Jim Doyle & Associates UPGRADE Selling® event with over 150 of our station clients, flying in from all over the country, to listen to yours truly speak.

After reviewing the injured leg x-rays at Urgent Care, I sent a message to our leadership team and Jim Doyle summarizing that, "...my leg is broken, in a splint, but the Atlanta show is still on. I have arranged for special airport terminal transportation and will even pack a knee walker which will allow movement around the platform. The doc was nice enough to prescribe pain killers to get me through the event until I can see an ortho doctor upon my return to Sarasota on Thursday."

That's the message that went out.

However, the message that circulated in our company, behind my back, was something like, "Yeah, right. John thinks he's getting on a plane with a broken leg to speak for 2 days! Everyone, please look at your schedules and calendar commitments. Is there anyone who has taught and mastered this content previously and has Monday through Wednesday open?"

It's a good thing the team *was* working behind my back. Sitting up in bed at 3am with a leg blown up the size of a basketball, it occurred to me that there was no way I was getting on a plane, let alone going to be able to navigate a stage for 2 days of speaking while the leg continued to swell with bones out of place.

Tom Ray, who seems to always have his travel bag packed at the ready, jumped in to take over Atlanta, and from the video I saw, he over-delivered for everyone in attendance.

In fact, 3 months of travel was pulled from my schedule and reassigned to Tom, Pat Norris, and Jim Doyle, almost simultaneous to us finding out the recovery for a leg break of this severity is 12 weeks of non-weight-bearing rest. That means no speaking travel. The recovery loophole, however, did allow me to call the office, check email, and make phone calls, assuming the pain killers allow me to carry on a coherent conversation.

While all of this was going on behind the scenes, I was thrilled to learn that we didn't have to cancel a single event, we didn't get one client complaint and, even more impressive, our revenue pacing was up year-to-year, all while the president of the company was mostly "unavailable."

Our team had passed the test.

What about you and your team? What if, hypothetically, you broke your leg tomorrow morning and had to be out of commission for 3 months? Would your business revenue increase, go flat, or decrease?

What this ladder accident proved to me is that a single, tiny split-second decision has the power to affect many weeks or even months of one's future. Preparing for these events is an entirely different strategy vs. when one is planning an absence for an expected event like an upcoming surgery or maternity leave.

The proper accident has the ability to take one out of their day-to-day, without the benefit of planning for the absence. That's where the power of building a bench comes into play.

In your absence, are there individuals ready to fill in for you and not only cover the business, but grow the business? Have they had enough "test-drive" opportunities to provide the confidence they'll need to face more difficult challenges? Do you trust them?

Recognize that your temporary replacement may not be a single individual. More than likely, it will be a number of individuals assuming different parts of your tasks, as they will continue to occupy their existing roles as well.

In the wake of an accident, all of these questions, and more, demand immediate consideration. And, given your tolerance for pain, you may not be in a situation where answers to these questions are easily concluded, unless you were pro-active enough to build a bench and plan a replacement strategy, anticipating that you could fall off a ladder tomorrow morning and break your leg!

CHAPTER 2

COACHING TO WIN

Winning is not a sometime thing; it's an all-time thing. You don't win once in a while, you don't do things right once in a while, you do them right all the time. Winning is habit. Unfortunately, so is losing.

-Vince Lombardi

MY FAVORITE "DIFFERENTIATE" STORY

If one expects to get a few minutes of discussion with the client decision maker(s), then positively sticking out among the crowded landscape of competitive sellers is an absolute necessity. I emphasize this thought in my TV station custom teaching days with a one-word summary—differentiate.

I often hear stories of sellers trying to differentiate with creative email subject lines, calling prospects before, after or during weekend hours, or even dropping off baked goods or event tickets to break away from the clutter and get noticed.

But my favorite "differentiate" story comes from star Account Executive Dave Elenkiwich in Minneapolis, Minnesota.

Dave writes:

Many years ago, working for another station, our News department did a story about the shortage of priests. The promotion department marketed the story through the TV Guide *and wanted to use me as a praying priest. In reality, I'm an average Lutheran, so go figure!*

At the time of this story, a couple of clients would not return my calls. I wasn't standing out (differentiating) from the rest of the Twin Cities salespeople. So, I bought a dozen TV Guides *with my picture and sent them to my clients with a 3M sticky note stuck to my picture with the following:*

"I often talk to God. Why can I not talk to you?"

Over the next few months, I sent TV Guides *to ten clients and six called me back right away. Two took my calls the next time I called, and two never spoke with me. I think those two saw through me!* What are you and your team doing to differentiate and get noticed by prospective clients?

THE LOWEST RATE DOES NOT ALWAYS DELIVER RESULTS

While searching for medical marketing updates, I stumbled across a marketing agency that specialized in the healthcare category. Feel free to shake your head in amazement as you read the below "pitch" from their website.

Media Buying... That Saves You Money

...We can get you on the air, on the Internet or in print, generating tremendous impact... for much less than you may think.

And, if you are currently advertising, take our Rate Challenge.

Send us your current schedule, if we can beat it, then let us handle your media planning and buying... giving you ongoing cost savings and the best guidance in the industry—with no additional cost!

Remember, **the media typically pays the media commission,** *and we'll typically save you far more than the cost of our fees.*

So, you'll usually pay less for the media and pay nothing to us.

One can only imagine the misinformation and questionable guidance that no doubt accompanies a conversation between this supposed experienced agency and a gullible healthcare decision maker.

Over the entirety of my career, I have yet to find a positive correlation between the lowest rate and results. In fact, I've witnessed quite the opposite. Agencies that build their foundation with an absolute lowest rate mentality tend to overlook higher priced opportunities that are much more demo targeted, with much higher audience deliveries and, as a result, higher ROI's.

The agencies with this mentality tend to churn clients at a much higher rate than an agency that focuses their buying strategy on client ROI's and sales revenue increases resulting from marketing campaigns.

So how can you help your AE's in this situation?

Make sure your sales stars create and maintain relationships with client decision makers. Agencies are never the economic decision maker. The client always maintains the power to dictate "must buys" to the agency, proving the importance for your sellers to maintain open communication with the client.

Lastly, make sure to teach your team to center their client decision-maker discussions not on rate, but instead on the importance of satisfying their client's need to push sales. If the client views your sellers as consultants instead of peddlers, they are less likely to be concerned about rate, and ultimately, will not be tempted to listen to an agency that touts their ability to get a lower rate. In this instance, rate is a non-issue.

THE NEXT SOUND THEY HEAR SHOULD BE A NUMBER

When you say, "I love you" to someone, what's the immediate response you hope to hear? My guess is that your expectation is some form of the same: "Love you," "I love you too," "I love you," etc. Any answer counter to that, or even a pause before the answer, would make one suspicious or concerned, or may even cause one to question the trust in their relationship.

That was the analogy I offered to a mid-market sales manager who disagreed with my belief on how to handle the most common question from the decision makers of prospective new, local direct businesses: "How much is a commercial?"

My suggestion? The next sound out of a seller's mouth should be a number. The sales manager disagreed, stating that there were too many variables to be able to quote a number.

I get it and was guilty early in my sales career of offering a long, drawn-out, multi-paragraph response before getting to the answer of the question with a number. But, over time, I learned that prospects build impressions of sellers the second of the first contact. They ask themselves, "Is this the one I want handling my hard-earned dollars? Can I trust this one?"

If an AE can't clearly and succinctly answer the "how much" question, the prospect may feel an air of distrust. It's the old suspicion of "the more talking without answering the question, the more someone must be hiding."

The conversation can get even more confusing when we consider the sales interaction with a local retail business owner. For example, in their world, someone may ask, "How much is this 2-inch screw." The response is simply, "Forty-nine cents." If this same decision maker asks your Account Executive, "How much is a commercial on your station?" They expect to get an immediate number. Instead, many sellers will respond with something like, "Well, that depends. We have various dayparts, with different programming that targets different demos. So, based upon the time of... blah, blah, blah!" Quite frankly, I don't blame a client who stops listening to this kind of response after hearing "...that depends."

How should the "how much is a commercial" question be answered?

Establish trust and credibility with numbers first, then it's okay to follow up with additional information to justify the number difference.

For example, "Forty to 5,500 is the investment range of our commercials." (Long pause to let the numbers sink in and to gauge response to both numbers. Their eyebrows may stand on end hearing the larger number. If not, that should be an indication for their tolerance of larger investment discussions. Note the word "investment" not "cost.") "Forty to 5,500 is the investment range of our commercials. As I'm sure you already know, the individual commercial price is established by audience delivery, demand on the inventory, and time of year. But, that's not anything you have to worry about. I'll make sure to match your budget to our digital and programming to satisfy your marketing need with a push of multiple thousands of eyeballs to your web, phone, and door."

In your next sales meeting, encourage everyone to begin their answer to each question in the meeting with a number. Then, have them take turns role-playing answers to the "how much" question. You'll hear many "aha's" and lots of laughs.

THERE IS SUCH A THING AS A CONVERSATION DO-OVER

Hard-charging, type-A personalities, of which I'm guessing there are a few reading this message, are sometimes accused of not listening or not paying attention. Many who hold a management title fall into this description.

The reality is that type-A personality brains are constantly processing tasks and self-talk. They tend to walk faster and more determined because they always have somewhere to go and something to do. When approached, these individuals have a split second of disorientation, as their mind moves from task-oriented self-talk to addressing the person who "interrupted." Sound familiar?

Often, the perceived interruption contains a topic of minimal priority for the manager, while simultaneously, being the most pressing issue for the individual asking the question. If you're like me, it's quite some time after the conversation when the realization hits that you were not as engaged with the individual as you could have been. You weren't in the moment. In those instances, wouldn't it be nice to get a "do-over?"

Well, good news! According to The Business Productivity & ADHD Coach, Nancy Snell (nancysnell.com), you can take back or add statements to previous conversations. One of my favorite techniques suggested by Nancy is to go back to the individual and state something like, "I've been thinking about our conversation and realized I didn't quite say what I meant to say when I said XYZ."

Try it and listen as the dialogue unfolds in this second chance do-over when you get to say what you should have conveyed in the first conversation.

My wife, Bridget, and I are the proud parents of three kids, all in high school. As of this writing, Evan is 14, Cara is 17, and Madison is 18. As I've been doing every morning since they were in grade school, I write a quote and slip it into their lunch boxes. There's no rhyme, reason or order to selecting the quotes for the daily deposit. Usually, they come from a list of my favorites; something inspirational or funny, or maybe a quote that has relevance to whatever is going on in their lives at the time.

Every year, as the summer break comes to a close, I hold my breath while asking the kids, "Is this the school year I should stop putting quotes in your lunch box?" Thank goodness, every year the answer has been the same, "No. We like the quotes. Keep doing it!"

Wow! The kids, my teenagers, actually like our daily "connection"!

That was, until Madison approached me. "Dad, I'd like to talk to you about your daily quotes," she said. My heart sunk. "Dad, we want you to keep giving us quotes..." Okay, heart back to normal rhythm. Madison continued, "...but, we'd like some different quotes. You know, some that aren't so funny, maybe some that don't involve 'blasts from the past' like Hannah Montana. Give us the leadership stuff from some of the big-time

45

motivators and speakers you always talk about."

My kids have grown up.

Unfortunately, as they've matured, my content—my attempt at delivering a motivational boost to their mid-day—hasn't kept pace with their maturity. As a result, I was "shooting below" their level of comprehension and desire. Apparently, this had been going on for quite a while. The kids were just too embarrassed to tell me. They didn't want to hurt my feelings.

Nearly a month after joining Jim Doyle & Associates, Jim shared an incredible statement with me during a discussion on writing proper content for our client presentations. He said, "Always make sure you are two chapters ahead of the audience." That's probably some of the best advice anyone has ever offered to me.

In any given room of sales professionals, there's a myriad of experience and talent levels. If one were to offer content that was rudimentary, again "shooting below" the comprehension level of the majority of the room, the individuals will check out and become frustrated, thanks to wasted time. Further, the speaker or teacher/trainer loses credibility.

The flip side is also true. If one were to offer content that was extremely advanced, "shooting way above" the average comprehension of the room, many will check out, thanks to confusion.

The key is to offer content that is two chapters ahead of the average comprehension in the room. Doing so will challenge the lesser experienced, while at the same time it will provide new thoughts for the more advanced participant.

That's why it's so important for you, as a leader, to consume, craft, and offer information, techniques, and strategies that are relatable and relevant to your sales team. Recognize—as I did not with my kids—that maturity levels change and your content had better grow as the individuals grow.

Understand that your personal effort at improvement is not a one-month obligation. This is something that has to be ongoing—24/7/365. The best leaders and managers recognize this and commit themselves to some form of daily education to ensure they're two chapters ahead of their teams.

So, what do you think? Does your teaching and training still motivate your team or are they embarrassed to tell you otherwise because, like my kids, they don't want to hurt your feelings?

A QUIZ FOR WORK AND LIFE BALANCE

My friend, Marty Grunder, is a fellow speaker and a pretty good business operator. Besides speaking and motivating audiences to action, he runs one of the most successful landscaping companies in the country. (http://www.martygrunder.com)

Marty is a champion of work and life balance,

which, if you're like me, can sometimes be elusive and seemingly never mastered.

Below is a recent short article from him that has me questioning the importance of some of my daily actions:

Every year around this time, I ask you the series of questions below and ask you to think about where your life and business are heading.

Ask yourself these questions again and see where you stand:

1. *When was the last time you personally saw each of your top 25 clients?*
2. *When was the last time you took an afternoon off and just went home to be with your significant other or your family? (If you tell me you don't have time to do this, you don't understand what it takes to be successful.)*
3. *What is the most effective way you have of getting new clients?*
4. *What was the name of the last business book you read?*
5. *Who has helped you be successful in the last year? Do they know you feel this way?*
6. *Can you run a mile without stopping? Do you weigh more or less than you did a year ago? When was the last time you went to the doctor for a check-up? (3 questions, I know, but good ones, eh?)*

My purpose is to make you think about what it takes to be successful. It's not just one or two things and it's not all about business.

The most successful small business owners are the ones that take a holistic approach to success. Business is part of it, family is part of it, and your personal well-being is the other part of it.

I hope these words have provided clarity on your priorities.

CHANGE YOUR MODE OF COMMUNICATION TO CHANGE THE OUTCOME

It was hard to hide my smile while listening to the star media seller express his frustration over his daughter—a typical "smart, lazy teen." The dad revealed how getting in his daughter's face to express disappointment whenever she randomly bombed a quiz never resulted in lasting outcomes.

In a last-ditch effort, he tried texting his daughter, letting her know how much he appreciated her hard work while she juggled a heavy class schedule. In a return text, the daughter admitted her shortcomings and promised she'd do better next time. Her text ended with, "I love you Dad."

The reason I smiled during this media seller's story is because it was so relatable and could very easily have been my own.

Over time, I have determined that my teenage

kids do not check email. However, being an over-50 dad, when the kids aren't available to speak on the phone, I prefer to communicate via email. It used to aggravate me that my emails to them went unchecked. Then, one day, I sent a text that got an immediate response from all three teens. Bingo! A different way of communication delivered an entirely different outcome.

The same can be said of managers to sellers. Maybe you're in a situation where it feels as though you're beating your head against the wall, repeating yourself over and over to individuals on your team. You're losing sleep because the outcomes never change. Unfortunately, unless you change, unless you determine a different mode of communication that is comfortable to the receiver, your desired outcome will never arrive.

It's not up to the individuals on your team to learn how to communicate with you. Instead, it's up to you to learn how to communicate with them.

To further complicate the situation, not every person favors the same mode of communication. Each could prefer a variation of methods, like in-person discussion, email or text. Some will need confirmation for clarity at the end of each discussion, others will respond to story analogies, while still others want to see expectations in bullet listings or spreadsheets.

I can't tell you which mode to utilize or how you

should communicate with each individual. What I can tell you is that the best leaders study to improve their interactions and are seasoned at recognizing when and how to break through with expectations and needed input.

HOW DO YOU RESPOND WHEN YOUR TEAM TAKES A LOSS?

"We got beat. So, we're going to move on quickly... We've identified things that have to get better, and we will, because that's what we do." These were the words of The Ohio State University head football coach, Urban Meyer, in a press conference immediately following the Buckeyes 31-0 loss to the Clemson Tigers in the Fiesta Bowl—the first round of the 2016 College Football National Championship Playoff.

Never before, in his 16 years as a head coach, had one of Urban Meyer's teams finished a game with a goose egg—a big fat zero.

In the darkness of adversity, real leaders establish themselves by discarding excuses, taking ownership of the moment, and putting the misstep behind them.

Coach Meyer did just that with his next statement, "Ohio State is *not* used to this. *I'm not* used to this and *we will not* get used to this. This is not going to happen again."

The message was delivered in such a deliberate

tone and pace that Buckeye fans and even non-fans knew that, under Urban Meyer's leadership, Ohio State would one day soon be back in the playoff picture and the outcome would be different.

How do you handle the situation when your team takes a loss? Maybe your team didn't keep pace with the market on the last revenue audit. Did you call a sales meeting to yell and scream, point fingers or maybe place blame? Or, did you take the hit, holding yourself accountable, before detailing the work that everyone in the room was going to put in to rectify the situation?

The direction you take and the style in which you convey your concerns are directly related to the ability to reverse your negative fortunes.

Like Urban Meyer, the best leaders understand this.

IS YOUR OPERATION WORTHY OF THE "NATION" NAME?

While watching an NFL game, I heard the reference for the first time: "Let's check-in on *Raider Nation,*" the commentator stated. The fans on the screen were going absolutely nuts! Virtually every one of them were clad in some sort of Raider silver and black, with painted faces and costumes reminiscent of the post-apocalyptic action film, *Mad Max: Fury Road.*

Raider Nation, indeed—a large mass of people bound by a common interest. In this case, they are die-hard, raving fans for their Raiders. Some in the Raider Nation are so over-the-top for their team that they have cemented their loyalty with Raider tattoos on their person!

It wasn't long after, that I started noticing the "Nation" title was picking up steam, crossing over to all kinds of pro, college, and amateur sports. For example, there was the NBA Los Angeles *Laker Nation*; the MLB Milwaukee *Brewer Nation*; the University of Oklahoma *Sooner Nation*; and finally, on a more local scale, the WBDT *Bumble Bee Nation*—a 5-to 8-year old, TV station sponsored, co-ed soccer team.

To be fair, not all of the teams claiming "_____ Nation" have winning records, nor do they have multiple thousands declaring allegiance to their team.

But, I'm a purist, and I say that in order to declare a team "_____ Nation," there has to be a track record of consistent winning—something that denotes what others have not, cannot or will not accomplish—for as long as the team claims "_____ Nation."

So, before you claim your team's industry superiority with a new "_____ Nation" title, the question I would like you to consider is "Are your actions worthy of the title?"

Are you consistent and the best in your market in your:

- mode of operation
- culture
- morale
- professional accountability
- plan to achieve the vision
- performance
- outcomes
- level of enthusiasm
- wins?

If you *are* consistent and the best in your market in each of the above, you *are* worthy of the "_____ Nation" title. The question you need to answer is "Next year, how will we build on the positive momentum to retain the title?"

If you are *not* consistent and the best in your market in each of the above, you are *not* worthy of the "_____ Nation" title. In this instance, the question you need to ask is "Next year, what will it take; what do we need to do to get there?"

The ultimate test to determine "_____ Nation" worthiness is to listen to your employees. Are the team members proud to wear their respective media calls? Are they thrilled to represent your outlet?

Finally, seek comments from your clients and community. What are they saying? Some form of "This individual, station, and/or company is different and I should listen to them" is a tremendous compliment and confirmation that you are on the right track.

Until then, keep an eye out for the ultimate in dedication—a media rep with their company name or call letters tattooed on their body!

CHAPTER 3

MANAGING FOR MAXIMUM PERFORMANCE

The greatest leader is not necessarily the one who does the greatest things. He is the one that gets the people to do the greatest things.

-Ronald Reagan

MANAGEMENT BY OBSERVATION

While doing some speaking prep, a phrase with which I wasn't familiar caught my attention—management by observation. The definition described this as management of employees by observing that they are present at the physical workplace during accepted working hours and appear to be doing expected work tasks.

It strikes me that short of replacing the word "work," this definition could be substituted as a description for babysitters. Unfortunately, there are still managers in our industry who oversee their operations or departments as though they're babysitting. Chances are you've heard them say something like, "I've got 3 kids at home and 9 kids at work."

One doesn't have to physically see an individual in action to know that the work is satisfactory or that it's even getting done. For example, if we watch our station and cable outlet channel(s) and there are no clips, bumps or dead air, we can assume the Master Control Operator (MCO) is present and doing a fine job of firing all the right buttons at the correct times. However, if the signal disappears and dead air fills the screen, or commercials are being clipped, we will assume the MCO is not present or not paying attention.

We arrive at these conclusions by observing the expected outcome.

The same applies to a sales organization. The best managers are leaders who track outcomes: how a seller is progressing in things like digital sales, new business sales, account shares, budgets, project sales, and churn. If a sales star is achieving expectations in all measured categories, does it really matter if they're at their office desk at 2pm on Thursday?

If you happen to manage by observation, you probably do care. However, if you're an engaged leader, you likely don't care when/why salespeople are in the office, as long as they're getting the job done. You recognize that you cannot create positive momentum with hard and fast rules that have the potential to slow down the effort of some on your team. They may need a bit of flexibility to achieve big revenue increases.

Please recognize that I referenced "some on your team," as there are always a few who are not meeting revenue expectations. In those instances, a deeper dig into individual sales processes, time management, and even some application of new rules is certainly in order.

THE FAST BEAT THE SLOW

The Director of Sales had a tone of confusion in her voice when she said to me, "I don't understand. We supply every AE with training and the latest and greatest sales tools. We're able to sell not one, but two, network affiliated stations and some of the best digital products in the industry. We have every conceivable advantage but still seem to lag when it comes to capturing substantial revenue shares in the market."

This DOS had proven herself as indispensable to the new big group ownership. She was obsessed with building the perfect team and had previously been given enough runway to make that happen. But now, she was under pressure to reap the revenue results of her vision and she was falling short.

It was obvious she was "managing" out of fear

and not "leading" with confidence. As a result, her sellers were overwhelmed with team meetings, one-on-ones, and a multitude of reports justifying the loss of money. In short, valuable sales time was used up and the competition was beating her sellers to the doorsteps of prospects.

It wasn't too long ago in business classes that you were likely taught "the big eat the small." That statement is no longer true, which may come as a surprise to you given today's business environment of big company consolidation.

In the situation with my DOS friend, she assumed that being big and fortified with sales tools was enough to win in the revenue game.

Instead of the big eating the small, think in terms of the "fast beating the slow." You see, one can have all the tools and advantages in the world, but if they lack motivation or a plan of action to capitalize and present those benefits, they can easily be beaten by a smaller competitor with fewer resources that gets to the prospective customer first.

The fast beat the slow. It's a great topic for consideration if you sense your team's revenue effort is falling short.

THE SECRET TO WORKING FEWER HOURS AND MAKING MORE MONEY

Every year, I look forward to attending the National Speakers Association (NSA) convention. It's a "train the trainers" opportunity that caters to thousands of speakers from around the globe. At this event, my brain gets re-energized for new ways of collecting, evaluating, and presenting relevant content. It's also a great place to network and catch up with some incredibly smart business operators.

Many members of the NSA are solopreneur speakers. As a result, they don't get paid unless they're on the road speaking. The more time they spend on the road, presumably the more speaking "gigs" they get and the more money they make.

At Jim Doyle & Associates, the company model is slightly different. There are multiple services and products that don't necessarily require going on the road to give a speech. Sure, I'd go on the road and speak, but the majority of the company's income wasn't dependent upon the number of speeches we'd deliver annually.

In a break-out session at one of the conventions, the conversation turned to the need to get more prospects in order to book more speaking events. I was directly asked, "John, how does your company actively increase speaking events?"

The group wasn't prepared for my answer. "We don't," I replied. "In fact, we'd prefer less time on the road and fewer speaking gigs." Silence and confusion hung in the air at our table. I continued, "We're shaping a formula that allows us to travel less, speak less, and, in general, work less, all while making more money!"

At this point, you might think I'm crazy. Of course, everyone wants to work less and make more money. But, that's simply a pipe dream. Or is it?

How many sellers do you churn on an annual basis?

Would you believe there are some sales managers who have shared with me that they lose more than 50% of their sales staff annually?

A company in this situation is on a forever treadmill, hedging their bets on personnel losses. Inside the building, there's no confidence among employees that any new hire(s) will survive.

And, outside the office? An outlet with heavy turnover lacks credibility, as clients have to "retrain" a rolodex of new account executives on their likes, wants, and needs.

I've encountered so many account executives who "undersell" prospects. Underselling is when an AE proposes a solution that lacks the proper investment to be effective. I call it, "Not enough peanut butter to cover the bread."

For example, if the absolute minimum monthly investment to be successful in an outlet's digital and television space is $5K per month, why would one undersell a client by accepting anything less than $5K?

As you read this, I recognize you may think the environment is too competitive to leave money on the table, regardless of the total. In some instances, I agree with you and feel it's okay to accept less than the monthly minimum to be successful, as long as an "expectations" conversation takes place with the client. The client needs to realize that anything less than $5K won't deliver maximum results, but that you will, for a short period of time, get very targeted in investing their less than $5K into your programming, products and services, and they will see minimal results.

However, before accepting their dollars, the client needs to agree to have a conversation to discuss converting their profits and dollars to at least the $5K level in 60 to 90 days, so they can experience incredible results enabling them to maximize their return on investment.

Too many times, this conversation doesn't take place, which results in a less than successful advertising campaign and a disappointed client and account executive. It's the root of the client objection, "I tried (TV, digital, your medium, your station, etc.) and it didn't work."

Soon, out of desperation, sellers begin to take *any* dollar total in an effort to replace their losses. If left unchecked, some AE's may find themselves exhausted, peddling packages or selling one-month contracts, for less-than-the-minimum dollars required to be successful. These AE's work more hours, call on more prospects, and generally make less money than their sales peers. Clients aren't renewing because they aren't getting results. Burnout begins to set in as these sellers start to question if what they're selling is capable of delivering positive results for their clients. Lastly, these individuals begin to question their career choice and their days under your employ become numbered.

The alternative is the AE who prospects for the right clients capable of investing the minimum monthly dollar figure to be successful. Or, if prospects balk at the minimum, these sellers make sure to conduct the expectations conversation and hold the clients to their promise. With a list of satisfied clients who are confident in the results they're receiving, renewals are an afterthought, referrals are easy to offer, and requests for budget increases and additional buys are easier to accommodate.

Sellers who don't undersell, when compared to those who do, tend to enjoy higher job satisfaction, stay in their positions with companies longer, and often work fewer hours while making more money!

YOU CANNOT ACCEPT SATISFACTION WITH MEDIOCRITY

Many years ago, JDA's company founder, Jim Doyle, had the pleasure of interviewing Jack Canfield, co-author of the *Chicken Soup For The Soul* books. The interview took place during the peak of the series' popularity. To this day, I remember a statement Jack made in the first five minutes of his conversation with Jim. It was profound, but at the same time concerning, especially when I thought about the truth in his words.

He stated, "A large number of individuals, maybe even the majority of the people we encounter on a daily basis, are satisfied with mediocrity." Wow, those are heavy words, describing a sad state of affairs.

It was not enough for me to accept Jack's comment by simply thinking of those people in my life—co-workers, family members, etc.—who fit this description. Instead, the credibility in this statement was confirmed after reflecting on how individuals arrive at a satisfied state of mediocrity.

At an early age, maybe as early as pre-school or kindergarten, we're taught the value of good grades. But, instead of touting how many answers one gets right, the emphasis is on how many answers are wrong. Students don't normally get checkmarks beside their correct answers. Instead, they get a test paper returned with X's for wrong answers, many times in red ink!

The conversation between classmates is, "How many did you get *wrong*?"

This scenario repeats year after year throughout the entirety of one's education. The negative reinforcement doesn't stop at the process of education. It continues to bleed into other areas of life. In sports, there are errors, strikeouts, fumbles, and fouls. In business, there are incomplete tasks, and missed goals and budgets. In love, unfortunately, there is divorce.

As you read this, you may think to yourself, "I hear you John, but those are all negative descriptors; there are positive ways to address each of those scenarios." You're right. In sports, we could say hits, touchdowns or scores. In business, we could talk about completed tasks and budgets made. In love, we could express the number of good years together before parting ways. However, that's not how the majority of society operates.

Many conversations, thanks to a lifetime of risk-averse living, are centered on what one *didn't do or accomplish* vs. the alternative. Individuals find comfort in mediocrity by not putting themselves too far out there, hanging back in the middle of the crowd, and going relatively unnoticed. This zone is safe and so doing just enough to remain in this space means one is less likely to suffer the humiliation of being wrong. These employees are not going to ask clients for major increases and they'll do anything not to rock the boat, as confrontation is risk.

As managers, we're sometimes guilty of adding fire to this way of thinking by giving those clinging to mediocrity reasons to stay there. We are consistently on the hunt for weakness and the team knows it. Have you ever caught yourself saying something like, "Nice new business order, but you missed your digital budget"? Trust me. Everyone on the team understands what budgets they're making and missing. Hearing this time and again from a manager, especially when the negative reinforcement is tacked onto a half-attempt at positive reinforcement, doesn't make the embarrassment of a missed budget any less painful.

The interesting observation for me is that many managers seem to revert to extreme negative reinforcement during times of adversity. They discount the multiple opportunities for positive conversations, capable of lifting performance, in favor of negative conversations that slow performance. Some managers may have even convinced themselves that this style of management is favorable because it holds the team accountable.

I disagree.

If your goal is to lift team members from mediocrity to greater performance, then you need to help them capitalize on their strengths, so much so that the strengths almost cancel out the weaknesses.

Positive reinforcement should never preclude negative reinforcement. A compliment like, "Nice new business order," should end on a high note. If you must discuss "missing the digital budget," then table the topic for a separate conversation. You should never deliver a negative after a compliment. Sincere deposits, recognizing effort, focusing on positive progress, and counting check marks instead of X's will encourage individuals on your team to break out of the comfort of mediocrity, act more confidently, and assume more risk. With risk comes reward—higher commissions for the seller and higher margins for your media outlet.

WHO IS YOUR DOCTOR'S BEST DRUG OR MEDICAL APPLIANCE REP?

Each year, Jim Doyle & Associates used to host live two-hour shows, in which we'd provide a deep dive into some of the TV industry's hottest revenue categories. One show was titled, "Code Red, Reviving Your Flatlined Healthcare Revenue." When JDA's Executive Vice President, Tom Ray, and I were discussing the goals and content of our broadcast, he revealed an interesting piece of information he'd discovered while doing research for the show. He'd found that the pool of pharmaceutical sales reps was continuing to downsize. Thanks to an oversupplied marketplace and continued industry regulations, the days of "armies" of medical sales reps stacking revenue has shifted to a limited number of specialized sellers.

The biggest nugget Tom uncovered is that most existing medical sales professionals are under contracts, which at its surface is not uncommon. However, Tom revealed, "The game has changed. Long-term employee contracts are no longer the norm. Today, many of these sellers are obligated to sign short-term, one- and two-year employment agreements, or as long as a new drug or appliance launch takes to complete."

I don't know about you, but looking for a job every year or two would get old really fast. Have you connected the dots yet? There are nervous pharma reps wondering what new drug or appliance they'll be selling next, and where, or even if, they're going to be able to secure another employment contract.

Not long ago, our television industry lost quite a few great sellers as a result of the pharmaceutical companies ramping up their recruiting of our stars to fortify their sales teams. Turnabout is fair play. It's your turn to provide a home for these medical sales stars. Likely, you will find that many of these sellers are smart, they close something on every call (agreement, next appointment, etc.), and they're capable of constructing and masterfully delivering an elevator speech. But the most important reason you should start filling your account executive recruiting funnel with pharma rep prospects is that they can get to medical decision makers—the very people your existing staff often cannot reach. Conversations with these decision makers is going to be key for you to capitalize on the HUGE advertising revenue opportunities that the healthcare category is expected to provide.

This information is useless without action. Within the next 24 hours, commit yourself to calling a few doctors who have cared for you in the last year and ask them this question, "Who are the best drug or medical appliance reps who call on you?" Then, reach out to the rep for a discussion as soon as possible, before your competition figures out this new sales hire secret!

A BEING "ON TIME" POLICY

An individual in the office asked about my policy for being "on time" for work. From my experience, this topic starts as a small speed bump but has the power to become a great divider if offenders are not corrected quickly.

I happen to be someone who *does not* believe in a blanket policy of comp time. If, for whatever reason, someone was in the office working until 9pm, that doesn't mean they're free to come in 4 hours late the next day. Notice I said, "blanket policy." That's because, unfortunately, there are individuals who will take advantage of situations and will squeeze out every bit of return they feel they are due, without regard to the successful completion of the company's priorities. These are often the same individuals who treat every sick day as extra vacation days.

All employees should be aware that an office has established hours of daily operation. As a result, the expectation is that everyone will be ready to produce when the doors open and are free to go home when the office closes. This is especially true of those responsible for welcoming morning visitors and answering phones. It's never a good reflection when potential clients are greeted with a "we're closed right now" recorded message— during business hours!

If you're faced with employees who are habitually late, you need to address the situation immediately. Why? Because other employees are watching. If the tardiness spreads, and it will, you will quickly get frustrated as unchecked arrivals move from 8:30am to 8:40am to 8:50am, etc. (By the way, if you're late, what message is that sending to the staff?) Your culture should define tardiness as the exception not the rule.

Many individuals will get leeway on the office hour schedule based upon their professional level of maturity, their commitment and performance, their travel and appointment schedules, and, in the case of sales, their production of revenue.

Many years ago, I was intrigued when a sales manager told me that one of his senior AE's was physically in the office about twice a week, usually to attend the sales meetings and pick up his mail. Upon voicing my concern, the manager explained that this particular seller lived well over an hour from the station. Despite the distance, this AE was consistently the staff's highest new business and local direct biller. Because of the sales pro's high level of revenue production, the rest of the team never questioned the manager's decision to allow the AE such office-hour flexibility.

I recall an opposite story of a not-so-pleasant experience with a senior AE who was a "great guy," but for some reason, he consistently arrived at the office 20 minutes late. On top of that, he had dropped to next-to-last on the team in new business billing. The AE made multiple promises to be on time *and* to increase new business, but nothing changed. Simultaneously, my credibility was in question with the rest of the team as they watched this seller continue to fall short and suffer no repercussions. Oh, did I mention that this individual had, on more than one occasion, stated how difficult it was for him to find time for new business prospecting because of his heavy agency and transactional workload?

When expectation turns to hope it's time to make a change. That's one of my favorite quotes and exactly what was called for in this situation— change.

This senior seller was put on a 90-day plan, which included monthly new business target minimums. I assured him there would now be plenty of time to prospect for new business as we were freeing his heavy workload by reassigning some of his agency and transactional accounts. Additionally, he was now going to be required to "punch-in" daily at the time clock, upon his arrival and at his end-of-day departure (as did our master control operators). He'd be allowed three late arrivals the first month, two the second, and one late arrival the third month. Exceeding those late arrival maximums would be grounds for losing another billing account.

I once referred to the meeting on the 90-day-plan with this long-time employee as, "the thud heard 'round the world," as in his chin hitting my desk in disbelief.

Did the plan work? Most definitely. In the next 90 days, the AE was late only one time and his new business increased 342%!

ADD A LITTLE SHOWMANSHIP TO INCREASE SALES

On July 4, 2016, Nathan's Famous hot dogs celebrated their 100th consecutive year of hosting the country's most prestigious hot dog eating contest. How do I know it's the country's most prestigious? Because the President of Major League Eating, Richard Shea, told the nearly 2.8 million viewers watching this spectacle that they were viewing history—the country's most prestigious eating event. The "World Championship" of eating, if you will. Mr. Shea delivered the message not just once, but multiple times, and with great fanfare, during the extended opening and competitor introductions.

At its essence, viewing an eating competition is pretty disgusting. Competitors shovel food into their mouths as fast as they can, trying to avoid reversals (inability to keep the food down), in an effort to be crowned the most gluttonous on the stage.

The constant dipping of hot dog buns into water to aid a quick food transfer is almost too much to view. Why then, you may be asking, do I continue to watch? I cannot look away because of Richard Shea. His showmanship could run circles around one of history's greatest promoters, PT Barnum. His eloquent descriptions of the events at hand make one believe that nothing is more American than a hot dog eating contest, and even more, it is the fiber responsible for the freedoms our citizens enjoy today!

In summary, Richard Shea believes in what he has to offer. He's selling the idea hard and I'm buying what he's selling.

Think about the sales challenges among your sellers. Why are some able to move programming, digital, or a promotion or cause that others on the team have difficulty selling? Could it be because they believe in what they're selling and their passion gets transferred to a potential buyer?

It used to drive me nuts when an AE would bring a completed commercial back to a client and say something to the effect of, "This is what our production department put together. It's their concept. If you don't like it, we can change it." NO! That kind of comment is weak and telegraphs to the client that the seller doesn't believe in the creative, so why should the advertiser?

Instead, sellers should promote the commercial just as hard as they sold the schedule and digital components, with a firm delivery—something like, "You're going to love this commercial. It has all the points we discussed and a special surprise call-to-action."

If you're disappointed in your team's lack of revenue results, maybe it's time to have a showmanship discussion at your next sales meeting.

After watching Joey Chestnut, a man, a mere mortal, eat 70 hot dogs in 10 minutes—nearly 1 hot dog eaten every 8.7 seconds—I realized that nothing is impossible!

In a hallway discussion at the NAB SMTE, a station manager brought up the topic of recruiting. More specifically, her concern was her sales manager's inability to find good sellers to fill their open AE seats. "Do you have any advice I could share to help him?" the station manager asked.

Do I?!!

Since recruiting is such a hot topic in our industry, I thought it might make sense to share a portion of my response on this topic with you.

If you're a manager who prides yourself on "gut" hiring decisions, I encourage you to change your way of thinking. Our "gut" provides a baseline instinct, but in today's business there's too much at risk—time, financial, credibility with existing staff—to make the wrong hiring decision. Testing is insurance against what could be a costly hiring mistake.

The hunt for the perfect candidate should begin with the exercise of listing the adjectives and descriptors of the ideal individual to fill your position. But don't stop there. Go to your best AE and ask him or her to do the same (without revealing your list in advance.) Lastly, go to the worst performer on the team—maybe someone who's on the bubble—and ask them to complete the same exercise. Then, take the time to compare all three lists. Very quickly the obvious "have to have" traits will surface, and likely, simultaneously, the traits you *are not* seeking will become clear. Don't assume you know what those are. (Thus, my suggestion to include input from your best and worst AE.) The bonus with this exercise is that things you *had not* considered important will become evident.

At this point, you will have all the information you need to craft the perfect new AE checklist and "help wanted" ad.

Speaking of ads... to get noticed and break through the industry clutter, you need to make sure your ad stands out like a green apple in a bushel of oranges. Resist the urge to advertise the usual "generate, manage, and grow revenue from local advertisers and agencies" lines. This does nothing to differentiate you from the competition. Instead, attract the right candidate by listing the specific tools you provide, the opportunities you afford performers, and the big-ticket or high-profile products available to sell, for example, specific sports, special events, etc. Don't forget to speak to some component of "fun." Over 70% of the industry's sellers are "Socializers." They like to laugh and celebrate. Your ad should contain something that speaks to the fun culture a prospective employee will enjoy.

Lastly, create a recruiting video that features all of the highlights I've previously described. Post it on your organization's airwaves, social media, and help wanted site. Additionally, post it to your personal social media. Create demand by using LinkedIn, Facebook live or Periscope to feature videos of office "fun" tours or show your well-known anchor or meteorologist encouraging viewers to "join the team." Many times, these videos gain momentum through "friend of friend" sharing, and the cost—FREE—fits any budget.

Challenge yourself to break the industry mold through creative and engaging "opportunity" announcements. By the way, waiting until you have an opening to pursue this strategy is too late!

FISHING FOR GREAT TV SELLERS

Do you know any fishermen who swear by a particular bait? They tell stories for days about how a particular bait or lure makes the fish practically swim up and beg to hop on the hook.

Now, think about the television sales industry. Have you ever been frustrated because your competition "lured" a big-time seller to their team—maybe someone you were trying to "catch"? Did the other media outlet land the star seller because they were a better fisherman? Nope. I would contend that, more often than not, it's the bait.

In order to be successful in today's mega-competitive television operations, you must build department benches. That involves your personal effort in networking, interacting with, and identifying star performers—those who possess an ability to advance your vision of never-before-experienced performance levels. And, all of this takes place *before* you have an opening.

During the time that you're actively trying to locate these stars, you should also add some ongoing shiny lures to your recruiting tackle box to differentiate your opportunities from the crowd of "also-rans."

The first lure is LinkedIn. Most management LinkedIn profiles are average at best. I'm not so sure that hurts you as a manager. Someone who wants to move to X location or is considering a career transition is unlikely to take a manager off of their call list because of a less-than-stellar LinkedIn profile.

However, it is important for you to take a look at your profile summary to ensure it speaks to what you do, what you provide or what you inspire. A few "tweaks" can make you a priority call over your competition as a candidate is putting together their job prospect list.

Remove as many "I" references as possible and refocus the description with new hires in mind. Make the description less about you and more about, for example, what your sales folks enjoy and what needs you're fulfilling for them as a result of being employed by your organization, and ultimately, you.

Confirm the things AE's in your region want

from an employer through questions of your current team or new AE's. Please don't assume you know.

If sellers want to be paid well, appreciated, listened to, involved in decisions, and challenged, then your profile summary should reflect that. Your summary might say something like, "As a star addition to The Lowcountry's CBS13, you will be challenged, your input will be valued and listened to, and you will be compensated extremely well for your hard work and effort."

Beyond LinkedIn, your recruiting tackle box should include social media lures like Twitter, Facebook, Instagram, Snapchat, and Periscope. We live in a video world. The fact that nearly every cell phone has a video camera makes shooting short videos a breeze. For efficiency, utilize a social media aggregator, like Hootsuite or TweetDeck, to easily share your videos across multiple platforms with one upload.

Record short clips of sales team "fun." That's important because as Socializers, a large majority of sellers have personalities that love to have fun and laugh.

Capture those moments from sales meetings, outings, from the sales pit, etc., and post them on your personal social accounts and on the station accounts. As an aside, with your phone, record one of your well-known anchors or meteorologists inviting potential sellers to contact you for a discussion. That's an absolutely great way for you to integrate your personal brand with the station brand to double up on the power of recruiting.

The last recruitment lure involves job "classified" commercials utilizing the power of your airwaves, cable, and digital products. Please don't feature the normal boring points like your opposition airs. Be bold and tell everyone why your opportunity is so special—the absolute best career opportunity in the market. Again, if you want to co-mingle personal and company brands, you should make at least a small appearance as the talent in the ad. Drive the point home with a great call to action like, "Contact me today to be on your way to the best career decision you could ever make!" But please, be honest with yourself and make sure it's TV worthy or your uncomfortable on-air appearance could backfire.

As we've already talked about, in today's business environment, it's no longer the big eat the small, but rather, the fast beat the slow. Differentiating from the competition, consistency in message, and frequency in exposure are the keys to recruiting success and hooking big employee upgrades. It's about being louder than your competition and getting noticed by the best workers in the market so that you are top of mind when the timing is right to add them to your team.

Happy fishing!

AN OBSERVATION OF DYSFUNCTION

If you've had the chance to attend a Jim Doyle & Associates Sales Manager's High Performance Boot Camp, you may have been lucky enough to enjoy one of our most popular keynote speakers, Roxanne Emmerich www.roxanneemmerich.com. She's a fellow Certified Speaking Professional, was inducted into the speakers Hall of Fame, and is listed by *Sales and Marketing Management* magazine as one of the 12 most requested speakers in the country. Her ability to transform negative workplace performance and environments into positive, results-oriented cultures is unmatched.

It's no surprise that someone with Roxanne's voice of experience is also a best-selling author. One of my favorite books of hers is titled, *Thank God It's Monday! How To Create A Workplace You And Your Customers Love.*

In the first chapter of *Thank God It's Monday!*, Roxanne suggests, "You have probably walked into a bank or restaurant or department store and thought, 'Yep. Dysfunctional.'"

In my travels, I have determined it only takes about thirty seconds to three minutes to size up the atmosphere when walking into a TV station or media outlet. Many "tells," or indicators, provide clues as to whether the building is full of motivation or if morale is suffering—before even having the first conversation.

Don't believe me? The next time you're a guest in an office, look for employee smiles and connection through eye-contact, listen for distant laughter, and watch how fast everyone walks. Are they in sync? Do they have a purpose? Are they engaged?

Then, have someone from outside your organization observe the same in your workplace. You might be surprised at the level of "dysfunction" taking place!

IT'S TIME TO THINK ABOUT REPLACING YOUR "GUT"

One Saturday, I was participating in some round table discussions with business owners, CEO's, and presidents. The topic that continually surfaced was the hiring of quality people. There was a consensus frustration that many new hires didn't work out and were let go after a considerable commitment of wasted time, effort, and money to train them. When prompted for further explanation on hiring processes, not one business leader stated they utilized employee testing. That was a surprise.

Why do managers feel that they don't need a test when considering new hires? The first response is always some form of "expense." I disagree.

How much does the wrong hire cost you? Forty-thousand, seventy-thousand, one-hundred thousand? If one stands to lose multiple thousands, it's almost laughable to think that a $50 to even a $1000 test is considered an expense vs. an investment. The "in the know" managers recognize employee testing as insurance against financial losses.

There's another issue that is sometimes overlooked when wrong hires are added to the team. Employees and sellers are holding you accountable for making the right decisions—to add the absolute best players to the team. Your repeated failure to do so negatively impacts your credibility, and your ability to lead will be questioned in hushed hallway tones—you know, those conversations between individuals that immediately stop when you get within earshot.

I ask you to consider replacing your "gut" with proven new-hire testing. Your checkbook and your team will thank you.

If you need test suggestions, I'm just an email away.

IS THE SELLER REALLY IN A SLUMP?

As a manager, there will be a day when you have to deal with a seller who's in a slump. But, instead of taking an individual's word, you should condition yourself to dig deeper into the situation, verifying that a slump does indeed exist and isn't the byproduct of misplaced priority management.

The fine line between perception and reality turns gray when sellers are unable to hold themselves accountable for the lack of activity leading up to a perceived slump. Maybe, the AE overlooked the required new business development while trying to close out the year. As a result, January comes and there's nothing in the funnel because nothing was put into it in 4th quarter. So, the problem isn't a slump, nor is it a January problem. It's a 4th quarter problem that created a deficiency in January. This explanation is exactly why it's not wise for sales teams to consistently sell inside a month. Doing so sacrifices budget-making opportunities in future months.

However, there may be times when salespeople are legitimately in a slump. But, from my experience, in challenging times, the slump is short-lived because great salespeople deliver. They recognize they can't think their way out of a slump. The only way to get out of a slump is for them to sell their way out. They spend less time in the problem and more time finding a solution to the problem.

On the other hand, average sellers spend more time in slumps. It could be that average sellers are in denial, or maybe their sense of what they need to accomplish gets clouded because of the setback.

Regardless, if you haven't already, you will encounter sellers in a slump. The key is to confirm its legitimacy or to reveal a problem caused by misplaced priorities several months earlier. If the slump is legitimate, be sure your sales star is living in the solution and not in the problem.

CHAPTER 4

SALES PREPARATION AND PLANNING

Give me six hours to chop down a tree and I will spend the first four sharpening the axe.

-Abraham Lincoln

LESS IS MORE

It struck me as funny when the VP of Sales pulled from his credenza a six-inch thick, three-ring binder with thirty-four sellable digital products. This was the presentation show-and-tell piece from which each of the TV group's account executives were expected to sell!

The irony of trying to sell *digital* products from *papers stuffed into a binder* was absolutely lost on this sales leader. However, that wasn't my biggest concern in this conversation. The sellers at this company were being taught to present from this binder as though they were walking a prospect through a menu. In other words, a prospective client was expected to sit and listen, as AE's droned on, endlessly detailing each-and-every one of the thirty-four digital product options.

I hate those restaurants where the server sits down at the table while taking an order. Can you imagine if they read every single item on the menu, out loud, discouraging your choice until they finished rattling off the entire menu?!

Many years ago, I read some interesting research that revealed no matter how many TV channels viewers had available to watch, they would only view about a baker's dozen with regularity. The 13-channel number stayed consistent, even though individual viewing tastes changed. For example, MTV may drop out of an individual's viewing preference, but it gets replaced with something like HGTV, still leaving about 13 "go to" channels.

In Joe Calloway's book, *Keep It Simple* (www.joecalloway.com), he writes of a Columbia University research study that took place in 2000, which confirmed that too many, or unlimited, choices is *not* a good thing. Researcher Sheena Iyengar set up a display of jams outside a grocery store. The display was rotated between having six jam jars or 24 jam jars from which to choose. The study was able to draw a correlation between higher sales and fewer choices.

How does this research apply to our world of

media sales? It can be summed up in one simple phrase: *less is more.*

Teach your sales stars to conduct a deep-dig conversation to identify a prospect's need. Then, they should return with a presentation, featuring limited options (2 or 3) max, which will satisfy the client's need. This limiting of choices will generate focus and minimize any overwhelmed or confused feelings a prospect may get from trying to decide between too many offerings.

OUR SALES GUYS WILL WEAR YOU OUT!

Years ago, as a TV station General Manager, I was hosting a group of clients on a tropical incentive trip. During the ride back from an excursion, one of the travelers mentioned she was thinking about getting a new car. She had been driving conservative four-door sedans for several years and was polling the group for their voice of experience on different SUV's she was considering.

A car dealership owner in our group, was within earshot of the discussion, and didn't waste any time getting to the point. He asked, "Have you looked at any SUV's on our lot?" The lady explained that she was simply in the research phase, wasn't committed to buying anything yet, but was curious if it would be premature for her to check out deals at the car dealer's store.

The car dealer took an extremely long pause.

Everyone in our group quieted to see what kind of "deal" he might be getting ready to offer the lady.

To the group's surprise, there was no offer! Instead, the dealer loudly proclaimed, "If you aren't sure you're ready to buy, don't step into our store because our sales guys will wear you out!"

We laughed until our stomachs hurt. Still today, when running into travelers from the trip, that is one of the first stories that gets repeated.

One can't blame the car dealer for being honest. His store is a high-pressure experience with sales numbers that stack up very well against their auto competition. He's a business owner in a category that caters to fickle buyers. Sure, his sales folks enjoy their share of repeat purchasers, however, most of their customer base is just as likely to go across the street to satisfy their price and selection needs. Thus, early in the training process, auto sales professionals are taught to not let the "up" walk out the door without buying.

Is the same true for the sellers in our industry? I don't think so.

First, ours is a multi-appointment process. Second, the foundation of our business is built on repeat customers. Those who come back and back, and back again, investing their hard-earned dollars by trusting the talents of your account executive and your company's ability to sell products through the power of your programming and digital products.

This is not a hard-sell opportunity. Please don't misunderstand my statement. After all, it's still sales, and as such, will often require a bit of objection countering and sales discussion pressure. But, sales success in our industry is no longer accomplished in one visit, slam-dunking a business owner on the package of the month. That's a short-term win and long-term loss sales strategy.

Your sellers should begin the process by anticipating a minimum of two or three appointments with each prospect before coming to terms on how the partnership is going to move forward. The multiple appointments are necessary to build trust and collect a thorough understanding of the business's needs. The information provides the foundation for a presentation where your AE will detail how your organization will fulfill the advertising prospect's needs and exceed their marketing goals. This sales strategy is the key to long-term relationships and multiple renewals— and does not "wear out" the client!

THE POWER OF GAME CHANGERS

It's no secret that the fastest route to successfully closing business is through the process of making meaningful client deposits—before asking for additional dollars. Some of the best client deposits fall into a category I like to call "game changers."

Game changers separate the winners from the

losers. Game changers establish the seller as an extension of the client's staff. Game changers lock up budgets from the competition.

My favorite game changer is to unexpectedly show up for a special retail sale day. What do I mean by that? Let's say you have a florist on your client list. The two biggest days for florists are Valentine's Day and Mother's Day. Let's say it's Valentine's Day. You show up at the florist's location unexpectedly, carrying breakfast for everyone—a superficial deposit—but then, you stick around. The business owner might ask, "Why are you still here?" You respond with something like, "Look, Bob, today is one of the biggest sales days of the year for you. You probably need an extra set of hands. What do you want me to do? I'll run the cash register, load flowers, make a delivery. You let me know." Wow! The client is going to talk about you for years to come for showing up and lending a hand on a special sale day.

My second favorite game changer is creating free vendor money opportunities. In other words, you're creating a win-win by finding free money for a client. Let me give you an example. At one of the stations that I managed we had a promotion where we threw out footballs on Friday nights at high school football games. On the footballs, we printed the client's logo and the station's logo. In this particular situation, there was a pizza chain in town and their soda pour was Pepsi. We went to Pepsi and said, "Look, we can get you exposure into all the high school games via your logo on all the footballs. In exchange, we're asking you to invest in a promotional schedule to support the event. Lastly, your biggest client, the pizza chain, will have a logo on the footballs. If you agree to pay for that, we'll make you the hero in this situation." So, what did Pepsi immediately say? "We'll do it. Where do we sign?" We then informed the pizza client that Pepsi had agreed to pay, not only for the pizza logo on the footballs, but also for the promotion of the football throw-outs. The client was thrilled. They didn't have to pay any more money. It wasn't co-op. It was free "found" money and it deep-seated our relationship with the pizza company.

I offer this topic as a contribution to your next sales meeting. Please share this article with your team and challenge them to come up with opportunities that deep-seat important client relationships and differentiate your outlet from the competition.

REVENUE OPPORTUNITIES SURROUNDING NATURAL DISASTER COVERAGE

My good friend and TV Network Executive, Russ Myerson, and I were having a conversation during a spell of California wildfires. I was concerned about Russ, as his home seemed to be right in line with the fire's direction. Thankfully, all was well with Russ and family and the fire was far enough away that it didn't pose a danger.

Russ described the outpouring of help that arrives during these wildfire events and how quickly the community embraces those arriving to protect life and property. We both agreed that the media serves an incredible role in providing information and coverage during these natural disaster events. However, they must lose an incredible amount of revenue with the wall-to-wall coverage that preempts the existing programming schedule and associated commercials.

Russ asked, "Wouldn't it make sense for stations to contract with an advertiser like Home Depot or a restoration company that would automatically be rolled into the natural disaster coverage, even if the exposure was something like a billboard? Wouldn't that be a win-win for the advertiser, reminding people in need of their services while providing a bit of revenue for the stations?" Russ had made a very astute statement. After all, stations agree to "standby" contracts for tow companies and auto body shops during school closings and snow emergencies. Doing the same in other weather-related or natural disasters would seem to be an easy transition.

Being a sales guy, I couldn't help but think of

categories of advertising after an event. For example, in Louisiana, nearly 40,000 homes were affected by flooding. Many of these homeowners had moved to central Louisiana, fleeing hurricane Katrina and are now faced with the familiar sight of rising water for the second time in their lives. FEMA—The US Federal Emergency Management Association—had set aside $33,000 to aid each homeowner without flood insurance. Russ proposed it might be a good idea for mobile home dealers to advertise during these times, as many families will need housing until they're able to rebuild. The FEMA dollars would be more than enough for a temporary mobile home.

Remember the news stories after Katrina about the sale of cars that were in the flood; information that wasn't disclosed to unsuspecting buyers? Car dealers in post flood areas would be smart to adopt an, "Our cars are certified flood free" position. Doing so would aid consumer confidence and differentiate the dealer from the clutter.

Encourage your team to look around your market. Chances are, similar opportunities are being overlooked.

SAVE TIME AND DE-STRESS YOUR TRAVEL

Annually, I log between 150,000 to 200,000 airline frequent flier miles. But every couple of months, just about the time I get as comfortable as is reasonable in an airplane seat, someone will say to me, "Excuse me, you're in my seat." In nearly every case, they're right, as I've mistaken the ticket gate number as my seat number.

Because this has happened to me, a supposed "seasoned traveler," more than once, I now utilize a mobile airline app that loads all tickets and shows the seat number in big font at the top of the screen. It's a welcome change from a single line of multiple numbers on paper tickets, especially in instances of tight gate connections.

This situation started me thinking about other travel tips and hacks that might be valuable for those of you in the media business, who find yourself viewing the world literally from 30,000 feet, probably more often than you'd like.

Do you ever get disoriented and forget where you parked your car upon returning from a trip? If you're a regular traveler, try to park in the same airport garage, or at least the same floor level, each time. Then, take a picture of where you parked. For extra backup, write down the row and parking slot number on your garage parking ticket or text the location to yourself.

Speaking of cars, to save destination rental car time, register for loyalty programs at rental car companies that don't require you to stop at a counter to pick up or return a car. It's extremely convenient to pass counter lines and go directly to a waiting car and claim it by simply showing your license at the exit gate.

If you use services like Uber and Lyft, make sure to update the apps to the latest software. Sometimes, an app upgrade with these services comes with a discount code for your next ride.

A good tip for paperless traveling is to electronically file all travel reservations in a folder on your phone. In addition, have hotels, rental companies, etc., send your invoice receipts via email. For other receipts like restaurants, take a picture and move them to your phone travel folder.

If you like to read during travel, instead of packing books, load them into a kindle or reader app on your phone or laptop. This saves briefcase space on the road and bookshelf real estate at home.

A portable backup charger is an absolute necessity to keep laptops, tablets and phones juiced and usable. This is especially true when flying "Coach" as most planes only offer charging outlets in First, Business, and Comfort Plus seats.

Speaking of backup, for a few years, I relied solely on my cell phone as an alarm clock—that was until the phone didn't sound the alarm thanks to an extended software update, including a shutdown and restart, precisely at the time the alarm was supposed to alert. Now, the hotel alarm clock and the front desk serve as backups.

When making your way through security, strive to get behind business travelers as they have likely mastered clearing TSA without delay. If you fly every other month or so, make sure to register for TSA PreCheck. If your airline travel is more often, it will be worth the investment for you to register for CLEAR, which promises minimal, if any, wait times getting through security.

Finally, if your flight gets delayed or cancelled, and at some point it will, have the airline's 1-800 help desk numbers programmed in your mobile. Then, when you join the long line of disgruntled passengers seeking rebooking, you can attempt to resolve your flight issue via the 1-800 number while holding your spot in line—just in case.

Here's a travel pro tip: do NOT unload your cancelled flight frustrations onto the only airline employee on the other side of the podium capable of booking you on another flight. I have seen so many people get sour with gate agents for delays or cancellations resulting from circumstances beyond anyone's control. Do you think the agent is excited about assisting these individuals?

Jim Doyle & Associates, EVP Tom Ray, has been known to fill his pocket from the hotel candy dish, expecting that during a travel hiccup, he'll make an airline employee's day by offering a piece of wrapped candy and smiling, while commenting, "You look like you could use a chocolate." Guess that explains why Tom sat in First Class and I sat in Coach our last trip!

THE KEY TO BETTER

The quote, "Knowledge is power," is something nearly all of us recognize and hold as true. During my speaking presentations, I like to play the contrarian with this comment, "Knowledge *is not* power. The *execution* of knowledge is power!"

My goal is to present a counter argument to get the crowd to consider an alternative to something they may have accepted at face value. Many in an audience are easily converted, as it's not a big leap to connect the dots that all the information in the world is useless—unless action is taken to put the info to use.

I was reminded of conversations on this topic while reading a blog post from Mark Sanborn. (www.marksanborn.com/blog) Mark is a fellow National Speakers Association (NSA) member and Certified Speaking Professional. He received the Cavett Award, the highest honor the NSA bestows on its members, in recognition of his outstanding contributions to the speaking profession. Mark has authored eight books, including, *The Fred Factor,* an international bestseller with over 1.6 million copies sold.

Suffice it to say, Mark Sanborn knows a thing or two about developing leaders in business. That's why I'm excited to share a portion from Mark's blog, which solidifies my belief that *the execution of knowledge is power!*

How Leaders Get Better Everyday

The Key To Better

...Nobody gets better "accidentally." Only wine improves with age without trying.

You don't accidentally improve significantly, reach the highest summits or make the greatest positive impact without intentionality.

How much do you want to get better? Teachers can teach you, coaches can coach you, and motivational speakers can pump you up, but it is what you do with the information that matters.

Ongoing improvement requires a process and is based on principles you correctly and consistently apply. The exciting thing is, when you're intentional and take action, the door to your future swings wide open. Your willingness to work at improving yourself is the secret to realizing your full potential.

You supply the commitment to getting better, coupled with the right plan and process, and your effort will start to pay off. It's well worth it.

Not only will it benefit you, but it will also benefit the people around you. Your customers will be happier. Your boss will be impressed. And your family will see you at your best—the spouse and parent you really want to be.

So, you have a choice to make. Are you content coasting along, content with the status quo? Or, are you ready to make your best even better?

Today can be better than yesterday, and tomorrow can be a little bit better than today. Choose to keep getting better and narrow the gap between how good you are and how good you could be.

Action: What one thing will you focus on improving today?

THESE TWO MARKETING OPPORTUNITIES, TOGETHER, ARE BETTER THAN ONE

Did you see the research from The Global TV Group titled, Online Businesses Booming On TV (6/4/18)?

The best summary of the research came from Gene McKay, publisher of the daily television industry e-newsletter, *Spots N Dots*. He writes: Figures from around the world show the extent to which online businesses are now investing in TV advertising, in some countries becoming the biggest investors in TV. The figures, compiled by The Global TV Group show that, from Brazil to

Germany, brands such as Amazon, Netflix, Expedia, and Airbnb are building their image, reputation, and sales through the reach and influence of TV. In 2017, digital-native companies— including brands like Amazon, Expedia, Wayfair, and eBay—spent over $5.9 billion on TV, representing a 10% increase over 2016. The report claims the investment trend demonstrates the strong relationship between TV and online, with viewers armed with Internet-connected devices able to respond to TV advertising immediately.

As of late, it's not unusual to see related headlines of major companies like Coca Cola, and Proctor and Gamble, moving millions of dollars from digital to television advertising. Please don't misunderstand—the trend in these types of companies is not a full cancellation of their digital efforts. Instead, they're cutting back on their targeted digital focus and shifting dollars to a medium with broader appeal and an ROI that consistently out-delivers other mediums—television.

As I dig deeper into the research, I can almost hear media outlet conference rooms around the country breaking out in simultaneous applause from TV sellers and boos from digital sellers. Please don't let this information promote a rush to judgement, as there's good news for both digital and TV sellers here.

Digital is here to stay. Advertisers continue to

perceive it as an effective advertising platform because it delivers results. However, the spit shine on digital is beginning to wear off, just a bit, as advertisers realize the power of TV cannot be ignored. This will become especially true as broadcast and cable companies continue to build their addressable TV plants, providing better reach against advertising targets and ad options at scale. In the *Wall Street Journal* article, "TV Ad Spending Shows Signs Of A Revival," (4/18/16) a Proctor and Gamble spokeswoman stated, "We see TV and Digital not as an 'either or' but an 'and.'"

Jim Doyle & Associates Executive Vice President, Tom Ray, uses the term "tradigital" to describe the powerful marketing one-two punch of digital and TV advertising.

JDA continues to promote the philosophy that TV account executives have to include digital in their TV marketing presentations, and digital account executives have to include TV in their digital marketing presentations. Neither opportunity should stand alone. They are better together than they are independent of each other.

Ultimately, good advertisers recognize the value proposition of both mediums and understand they can't do without digital or television. The debate is finding the right mix between the two.

Have you armed your sellers with the knowledge and understanding to help these advertisers?

The man and his son-in-law had equal ownership in the small car lot, complete with an in-need-of-repair trailer that served as the sales office. The inventory was inconsistent—maybe two dozen units—with *No Money Down* and sample monthly payments displayed in white liquid shoe polish on the windshields. Thanks to the hand-painted sign to the left of the trailer, *Guaranteed Financing Regardless Of Credit*, I had a pretty good indication of their target buyer.

The lot was located diagonally across the street from a shuttered auto manufacturing plant that had previously employed thousands. Predictably, the plant's early 1990's closing had crippled the economic momentum of the community. This resulted in empty houses, empty strip centers, and a mass exodus of the hard-working unemployed, seeking fortunes elsewhere.

That's probably why it took me over five months before deciding to stop and speak with the owners of the car lot, despite driving past the business two to three times daily, during commutes between downtown and the TV station.

The owners were more than receptive to my request for an appointment and stated that no one from TV had ever stopped in to discuss advertising. I can't say that surprised me.

104

What did surprise me was the substantial margin these two were making on cars from the auction... to their lot... to the buyer. The high margin meant their whole monthly TV advertising investment would be covered after selling only *four* or *five* extra cars.

After the second appointment, inside of two weeks, their commercial hit the air, rotating heavily through daytime talk and court shows. Near the close of the fourth day of commercials, the son-in-law called me, excitedly yelling into the phone that he was headed to the auction for the second time that week because they were running out of cars!

By the second month, they'd posted 35 units sold, which was more than double their normal month. They added phone lines and employees, and even built a nice sales lot office to replace the trailer. From there, sales continued to grow, as did their marketing budget and my account executive commission, which averaged about $1,400 a month, every month, for nearly three years, just from this single account!

I told this personal experience story of the "diamond in the rough" car dealer to a room full of AE's during a sales meeting. Their large market station was in the middle of change and they were loaded with excuses. Nearly the entire sales team had built their sales success on the backs of transactional accounts.

Unfortunately, transactional business is an uncontrollable that's not keeping pace with industry expectations. As a result, corporate staffs are pushing their stations to locate controllable dollars, also known as "local decision-maker" dollars, to offset the transactional losses. That was the new expectation of this conference room of AE's, and they were having difficulty with the change. Sound familiar?

In this sales meeting, when the manager asked for a status update on particular prospects, each AE provided their own version of "I reached out and they didn't return my voice mail or email." Then, one seller spoke up with a statement that likely everyone in the room was thinking when it came to many of the local prospects they'd been tasked to call. She said, "No, I haven't called them. They only have one location and probably can't afford us."

Wow. So, now it was out there.

As the sales team nodded their heads in agreement, the sales manager shook her head in disagreement and said, "I'm not saying you should spend your time collecting $500 accounts. However, you might be surprised how one call or visit can confirm or dispel your suspicions of a business's financials. You need to learn to give the prospect the opportunity to say, 'No.'"

Upon finishing my story with the staff, I recalled how ironic it was that a competing TV station was located only seven blocks from this car lot. I was glad no one from that station had thought to give the dealer "the opportunity to say no" before I did!

ARE YOU GUILTY OF UNLIMITED WEEKLY MEETINGS?

Did you know that primary care doctors spend up to 40% of their time on non-medical related issues? Minutes stack up as things like insurance reviews, electronic medical records, pharmaceutical rep meetings, and human resource issues prohibit the doc from practicing what they studied all those years to become, and ultimately, what they get paid to do.

Allow me to bring the question a little closer to home. What do you think your account executives say when I ask how much *non*-selling time occupies their day-to-day? 10, 20%? Not even close. Consistently, the response is *over* 50%. More than half of their time is spent on non-selling tasks! How can anyone maximize their sales opportunities when so many non-selling priorities take precedent over the core of why you hired them?

So, who's to blame for this situation? Of course, the seller has to assume some responsibility for their actions and their lapses in focus or chasing "squirrel" moments. However, it's not uncommon to hear *your* name, as a media manager, thrown into a sentence of blame—specifically, the time wasted in your unlimited weekly meetings.

Managers of television organizations today are scheduling way too many meetings. There are now all forms of mandatory meetings for your sellers: training, sales, digital, promotion and branding, production, new products, programming, book breakout, general station, planning and strategy, corporate, and on and on and on. I was even told a story where a manager still hosts mandatory *daily* morning <u>and</u> *afternoon* sales meetings. That's twice a day, five days a week, before adding in all other staff obligations!

To add to the silliness, many of these scheduled get-togethers lack agendas and organization. As a result, each interruption to the day drones on, making it difficult to consistently schedule appointments around the meetings, as no one can forecast an end time.

Your job is to remove roadblocks that prevent your sales stars from maximizing their sales opportunities. Time, or waste thereof, is a major roadblock. So, it's incumbent upon you to minimize these interruptions.

My suggestion is to schedule a maximum of *two* meetings per week: a sales/business meeting and a training/teaching meeting. If you need to add a mandatory meeting, above your regularly scheduled *two* meetings, then cancel either the sales or training meeting for that week. You should obligate your sellers to no more than a couple of hours a week in these sessions; an hour and a half for the entire week would be better.

But how?

The best time-saver is to make sure each gathering has a clearly written agenda and outcomes. Once the meeting outcomes are satisfied, the meeting is over. This will stop everyone from filling time just because the schedule has been blocked for an hour.

On occasion, consider switching conference rooms or locations. Alternate individuals who lead the meetings. Switch the chairs around so that attendees have to sit in an unfamiliar order. Host a standing meeting. All of these tactics remove the familiarity that tends to contribute to the longer duration of meetings because everyone gets too comfortable.

Take stock of the attendees. Maybe, not everyone needs to be present. Go for a walk if you're conducting one-on-one or two-on-one sessions. Not only will you reap physical benefits, the shoulder-to-shoulder posture is preferred for building agreement vs. the adversarial opposite sides of the desk sit-down.

Lastly, consider gathering your team thirty minutes or so before business hours. Sure, a few will be less than thrilled with the change, but from my experience, the uninterrupted time without office "distractions" in the background tends to increase focus on the priorities at hand.

GOOD INTENTIONS ARE ADMIRABLE, BUT...

He was standing across the room at the cocktail party, the same drink and the same laugh that I'd become accustomed to recognizing at these events. For the purpose of protecting the guilty in this story, let's call him "Steve."

Steve is a great guy. I've enjoyed getting to know him the last few years as I've been traveling the television industry speaking circuit. He's a seasoned television station sales manager, who is seemingly on every industry invite list; gatherings courtesy of the National Association of Broadcasters, State Associations, digital confabs, group ownership meetings, and even social events.

Thinking of Steve keeps my speaking content fresh and relevant, as he comes to mind every time I sit down to write a speech. "What if Steve is there and he's heard me speak about this stuff before?" I ask myself while gathering presentation-supporting documents.

So, you can imagine my surprise when his regional manager slipped by expressing her frustration to me that Steve's sales team(s) have made budget only one1 of the last seven quarters.

Wait, what?! Nobody comes close to draining ink pens like Steve. With each speaker and topic at these events, it appears he's capturing every word and concept. His effort would put the most detailed club secretaries to shame! Armed with that kind of knowledge, how can Steve's teams fall short of budget so consistently?

It was time for a fact-finding mission. During the next conversation I had with Steve, I asked,

"Have you broken down the average order, number of new business calls, and closing percentage with each AE?

Have you established the monthly minimum dollar amount that clients need to invest in your brand to be successful?

Have you been able to minimize sales burnout by getting rid of the "package of the month"?

In summary, he was on a rapid-fire hot seat for answers to a lot of the things I'd presented at these meetings—the very things I assumed Steve was diligently recording in his notes.

As we spoke, it became apparent that the capturing of the info wasn't the issue. Steve had every intent to turn his volumes of notes into sales performance success. Unfortunately, after every show, the return to the minutia and "office priority of the day" overshadowed any intent to make positive change by incorporating newly learned information.

Steve's notes were saved in a couple of three-ring binders, sitting on his office credenza, waiting to be referenced when there was more time... someday.

I have never heard a manager say, "Yea, 'someday' is here! Time to pull out those projects we've been saving to fill in our free time!" OK, a bit ridiculous, I know, but the point is that despite good intentions, those notes are never going to see the light of day and I think that deep-down Steve knows it as well.

This situation isn't that uncommon. If you know someone going through something similar, it's okay to push them a bit to understand the reality of inaction. They deserve congratulations for taking the notes and organizing them for future reference. However, if the process stops there, that's only about a third of the job. The final two-thirds comes in the form of the execution of the knowledge. The action, or the execution of the knowledge to positively affect the outcome, is the power.

Steve and I discussed a few tips for turning his notes into action. For example, concentrating on no more than five major concepts per each event he attends. He'll likely capture dozens, but by prioritizing and focusing on only five major concepts, the task of putting each into action for positive change isn't as overwhelming.

Once the five are completed, if he's hungry for

more, he can simply go back to his notes and pick additional concepts to add to his operation.

I suggested to Steve that, just like goals, as each idea is incorporated it should have a "finish by" or end date. Also, the anticipated outcome of each addition should be defined. Doing so will confirm or deny the success of the effort.

Lastly, I encouraged Steve to delegate action steps. The expectation that in today's multi-platform business, a single individual can achieve 100% in every measurable silo, is almost laughable. There's no shame in passing a bit of the responsibility to the team.

One of my favorite management strategies is to make category specialists of individual sellers. They're accountable for reporting progress to management and product or program availability to team peers. This not only alleviates some of the manager's stress, it also provides an opportunity to build a future management bench by observing how sellers respond to the mini-leadership roles.

I have no doubt that Steve will "get the barge turned." He learned that it's not only okay, but necessary, to pump the brakes sooner rather than later in order to uncover why progress isn't moving in the desired direction.

Ultimately, Steve now understands that good intentions are admirable, but the failure to take action on those intentions is counterproductive.

FIRE TRUCKS AND SALES

A local sales star was concerned about renewing client contracts because the competition was wallpapering the market with charts and graphs detailing her station's recent ratings slide. "What can I do to counter the competition and make the client want to continue to do business with me?" she asked.

My answer is always going to be the same, regardless of whether the seller is backed by huge ratings or no ratings. The key to renewals is to build a relationship with client decision makers through differentiation.

Why are fire trucks painted a bright color and have loud sirens? To make them stand out, make them get noticed among the sea of vehicles, so cars get out of their way.

The fire truck description is analogous to the media sales industry, or any sales environment for that matter. To be successful, to establish long-term relationships, one needs to understand and master the importance of "standing out" among an ever-increasing crowded landscape of media sales competitors. They have to differentiate.

To help the star seller, I offered the below bullet points on how to differentiate herself to increase the chances that clients would be comfortable repeatedly investing their hard-earned marketing dollars with her.

114

- Provide premium service and sincerely deliver more "business love" than competitors.
- Under-promise and over-deliver.
- When you do over-deliver, make sure to professionally get credit for the effort.
- Establish a Return On Investment (ROI) with the client early in the process to manage expectations.
- Consistently provide deposits to reinforce your genuine interest in the advancement of the client's business.
- Remember, doughnuts, tickets and t-shirts are okay when it comes to deposits, but only from time to time. They shouldn't be the foundation of your client deposit and service plan.
- Continue to let the client know how important they are to you and how much you appreciate their business through written and verbal *sincere* thank you's.
- Make your client feel special with a management "thank you" drop-in or a one-on-one management appreciation breakfast or lunch.
- Strive to make the client perceive you as an extension of their team.
- Establish a "we're in this together" tone in the relationship.

By no means is this an all-inclusive list. For a fun sales meeting exercise, add to the list by encouraging suggestions from your sales team(s). Then, encourage them to utilize these suggestions as the foundation of their differentiation plans and they will likely be pleasantly surprised when many local client contract renewals become after-thoughts.

DON'T OVERLOOK THE POWER OF A NAME

My wife, Bridget, and I were driving to see our oldest daughter, Madee, play in her last college rugby game of the season. Often, attending these games means pulling out the GPS and routing to college campuses we have yet to visit.

Exploring unfamiliar territory can be good *or* bad. Good in that you see places you've never seen, but bad when hunger enters the equation and agreement upon which unfamiliar restaurant to stop at seems impossible.

This is a situation when smart marketers— your prospects—can win.

Imagine you're hungry and find yourself in an unfamiliar neighborhood. Would you rather eat at "Bob's" or "Bob's Grilled Burgers and Shakes"? Unless you're vegan, or eating keto and it's not your cheat day, you probably picked the "Burgers and Shakes" title. Why? Bob's is the same place and the same food, no matter what it's called. But to draw in those unaware of how good the food is, the business had better be called something more than just a generic name. Otherwise, how would those not in the know, realize that Bob's is a restaurant? "Grilled Burgers" brings to mind thick, juicy, and satisfying. If your prospects want to sell to the masses, their names should corner the market with satisfying recall.

It's not just the restaurant business. I lived in Montana for a couple of years and drove the same route, passing the same businesses from home to office every day, sometimes multiple times a day. One day, I needed a haircut before heading to the airport. Unfortunately, a time crunch prevented me from driving across town to my normal barber. So, I asked around the office for some "local to the station" barber recommendations. Two people quickly recommended a place called "Tony's."

"Where's that?" I asked. In an almost laugh, the response I received was, "You know... Tony's. It's six blocks from here. You've driven by it every day for the last year and a half!"

Who knew that "Tony's" was a barber shop? The outside simply said Tony's and seeing inside while sitting at the intersection was almost impossible thanks to the heavily tinted shop windows. If Tony were a smart marketer, he would have added "Barber Shop" or "Haircuts" to clue in the clientele *not* in the know. As a result, Tony lost what could have been a couple of years of haircuts from me. In addition, if the experience was positive, how many more potential customers would I have told about Tony's?

So, as Bridget and I were driving to the game and doing the "I don't care, you pick *or* I'm not in the mood for that *or* we just ate that two days ago" dance, a sign came into focus that we had never seen. The restaurant was called *"Which-Wich?"*. But that was not the bait that made us turn into the parking lot. It was the secondary title claiming, "Superior Sandwiches." Without such a title, "Which-Wich?" would have been another unknown to which we likely wouldn't have given a second thought while passing. But because of the name *Which-Wich? Superior Sandwiches,* we gambled, went in, dropped forty bucks, and totally enjoyed the visit. Then, at the rugby game, we told at least a half dozen other visitors to make sure to check out the shop before they left town.

Lastly, I recognize there are business owners who think everyone knows who they are and what they do. Maybe they have a crazy business name that has nothing to do with their business and have been successful despite the marketing disconnect.

I suspect that's probably the kind of debate that took place many years ago, in a conference room located in a non-descript building in Seattle. Maybe that's why today, virtually every time one sees the name Starbuck's, despite the popularity of the brand, it is followed by the word "Coffee."

Use A Script To Increase The Odds Of Getting Voice Mails Returned

I received a voice mail from someone who wanted to sell me the latest in "proactive breach hunting" software. The caller continued to stumble through his script, "...in today's 'assume breach' reality—the new battleground is inside the perimeter. Malicious actors thrive in undetected and uninterrupted dwell time, and you need new strategies and tactics."

As the voice mail continued, it was apparent to me that this individual was relatively new to the "dialing for dollars" game. It must have been his first week. It sounded like he was handed a script and told, "When you get their voicemail, because you always get their voicemail, say this."

The message didn't flow, it lacked enthusiasm, and further, it left me scratching my head, wondering what in the heck is "proactive breach hunting software," why would I need it, and why have I spent so much time listening to this poor voicemail pitch?

The seller lacked passion. He was simply reading words from a page with no emotional connection.

Do you think I returned his call? Absolutely not!

At Jim Doyle & Associates, the philosophy was that every seller, regardless of experience level, should have a script to keep them focused on the intent of their phone prospecting. However, the script should be practiced and read enough times that the voice mail becomes conversational and doesn't sound like one is reading from a script.

For example: *Hello (furniture store owner) Mrs. Watson, my name is John Hannon from WAVF-TV. The reason for my call today is that I've learned of some incredible marketing ideas that are helping furniture stores across the country substantially increase their sales. I don't know if that would be anything you're interested in, but if you are, it would be my pleasure to share them with you. You can reach me at john@johnhannonmedia.com* or 777-7777

If you've covered this topic in your sales meetings, you've probably been hit with the question, "We're getting the appointment based upon revealing promised ideas that will increase their sales. Won't the prospect want to hear those ideas in the first appointment?"

I can understand that concern, but your stars need to realize that giving away ideas in the first meeting removes all leverage in the sales process. When questioned, teach your Account Executives to respond with something like, "Before I can share these ideas with you, I need to understand your business challenges and your thoughts on growing your sales. Then, assuming my ideas are a fit, I'll happily share those and an overview addressing your challenges and sales growth."

The first meeting is strictly about understanding the client's needs. The second meeting will reveal the multiple products and services capable of filling the prospect's needs.

However, none of this happens unless a seller's voice mail is compelling enough to get the phone call returned.

It's not uncommon for managers in our business to encourage sellers to monitor competitors for prospective "new" advertisers. The conventional thinking is that if a client is already advertising with another station, they believe in the medium and are "low-hanging fruit" for adding additional stations and station products to their marketing mix.

While this method of prospecting may be true, there may be an even more profitable prospecting opportunity being overlooked—current clients on your station or in your digital space.

If someone is a loyal advertiser, it's likely they're pleased with their advertising choice, as they're having success. If it weren't working, they wouldn't be advertising in the space. Ask your sellers to start paying attention to what local businesses are advertising on your air or in your digital space right now. They're doing it because it works!

If somebody is getting results, what does it say? It's likely that other people in the category can get results too. So, if your sellers discover three or four roofing companies on your station, that should be an indicator that your products and services are successful for helping advertisers in that category move product. As a result, there's probably another dozen or more in the market who aren't currently being called on.

Asking the question, "Who else in this category

can I go after?" is a great way to freshen a seller's new prospect call list.

IS THIS HOLIDAY ON YOUR SEASONAL SALES CALENDAR?

One night before heading to bed, I was conducting the obligatory nightly ritual of running the remote through the meat of the television channel spectrum. A graphic over a CNBC story caught my eye. According to the National Retail Foundation (NRF), Halloween spending that year, was projected to reach a new high of $9.1 billion (that's with a B!) topping the previous year's record consumer spending of $8.4 billion for the holiday.

Retail outlets anticipated that each consumer would spend an average of $86.10 on candy, decorations, and costumes. Greeting cards, a relatively new Halloween-related category was projected to account for an astonishing $410 million dollars spent by shoppers!

"Halloween is almost here and I can't wait—for it to be over. I don't like Halloween nearly as much as I did when I was a kid. At my age, when you dress up and go door to door, people call the police. So, I just dress up and stay home, but I make the trick or treaters give me one of their treats for one of mine. It teaches them vital business skills."

-Dale Irvin, Professional Summarizer

(www.daleirvin.com)

According to NRF, 48% of adults participate in wearing costumes, with witches and animals being the most popular.

Halloween consumers are seeking online and in-store early-bird promotions. But your sales team can't wait until September to call on this opportunity. This holiday should be on your seasonal sales calendar to make sure your sellers are on this fast-growing advertising category *early* in the year.

CHAPTER 5

WITHOUT CUSTOMERS YOU HAVE NO BUSINESS

No business can stay in business without customers. How you treat—or mistreat—them determines how long your doors stay open.

-Harvey Mackay

CLASSIC CUSTOMER SERVICE 101

It was a long day of plane-hopping to Dallas, Texas, the night before I was to speak at a group event of television general managers. I had already determined that a quick shower and early bedtime were on the agenda after checking into the Omni Hotel.

While sparing you the details, suffice it to say that this day was one of those days when seemingly everything that could go wrong, did go wrong. So, it was no surprise that my attempts to turn off the shower were inadequate as the faucet got stuck, wide open, spewing gallons of hot water down the drain.

I called the front desk, explained the dilemma, and, no exaggeration, inside of three minutes there was a knock at the door with an envelope delivery from a hotel employee. Inside the envelope was a card with this message:

Good Evening, Mr. Hannon,
I apologize for the matter of your shower leaking and have dispatched an engineer to fix this for you. Please let me know how else I can help.
Also, as an apology, you'll find a food and beverage voucher in this envelope. Enjoy your night. Thank you. -Taylor, Omni Hotels & Resorts

Immediately, upon reading the note, there was a second knock at the door. This time, I was greeted by the maintenance engineer. After a few seconds of "wrenching," he apologized, stating the issue would not be resolved tonight and he was going to call the front desk to have me moved to another room.

As I began to process the inconvenience of packing and moving all my "stuff," there was a third knock at the door. This time, two bellmen entered and proceeded to pack all my belongings onto a cart, politely refusing to allow me to carry anything. They escorted me to a new "upgraded" room and even turned on the shower faucet to fend off any still lingering fears from the broken faucet experience!

Eleven minutes was the total time for the entire process to play out: broken faucet, apology note, maintenance work, pack, move, unpack, and finally, my head on a pillow in a new, working faucet room.

The Omni team made a rose out of a thorn and secured a lifelong hotel customer by acknowledging the issue, apologizing profusely, attempting a fix, having a back-up plan, and overdelivering at every step of the process with a commitment to speed and minimal inconvenience to the customer.

It was classic customer service 101, something that so many organizations cannot or will not deliver. For some, these actions are innate, but for the majority, these actions must to be taught and reinforced from the top management tiers.

It was so great to be on the receiving end of premium customer service. Do you think clients of the media outlets in our industry would say the same thing?

YOU MUST STAMP OUT SMALL THINKING

During the end-of-year holiday season, our family has followed a semi-tradition of arranging a vacation to celebrate Christmas and bring in the New Year. For one of our more recent holiday vacations, the family unanimously picked a return trip to Hawaii. Our 50th state is always a great destination, regardless of which Hawaiian Island(s) one picks.

The many miles of beachfront are accompanied with mild temperatures and incredible sites. Tourism is the largest single contributor to the state's gross domestic product, representing about twenty-one percent of its entire economy. With nearly nine million visitors to the islands annually, the hotel and resort employees know how to deliver on dream vacation experiences. But, then again, no one is perfect—every time.

This wasn't our first stay at this particular Hilton property. In fact, we chose this resort again in part because of the impressive guest treatment and care from the hotel staff. On previous trips, "no" didn't enter the conversation. Every request resulted in an opportunity for over-delivery. "Of course, Mr. Hannon, let me see if I can get you a late checkout... Here are a couple of extra towel cards, just in case... Headed to the beach? You'll need some extra waters. Please, enjoy these, on us!"

However, that was not the case with our last stay at this Hawaiian resort. Despite being a Diamond member (the highest loyalty rewards "road warrior" category in this hotel chain) our vacation was ripe with employee apathy, a tone of disregard, and what I refer to as, "nickel and diming."

I should have known something was up when we arrived at the property and *not* one bellman approached to help with our six bags. Maybe they assumed our three able-bodied teens were more than capable of dragging luggage?

My request for a late checkout was met with an abrupt, "We can't honor a late checkout this week." There was no, "Sorry," or even an attempt to fake an effort by checking a computer screen.

There were too many, "you've got to be kidding me moments" to explain here, but I do have to mention the icing on the cake move that I am absolutely convinced the Hilton brand *could not* endorse.

My son, Evan, and I spent over 4 hours in one of the resort pubs watching The Ohio State Buckeyes football team beat the daylights out of USC. All the while, we placed order after order of nearly every appetizer offered on the menu. We added a couple of fountain Cokes, and at the encouragement of the server, enjoyed multiple refills each time our glasses neared empty. When the bill arrived, besides the $90 in food, there was a drink charge of $24—for *six* Cokes at $4 each.

You could have knocked me over with a feather when the server didn't blink before responding to my inquiry of his mistake, "I should have only given you *one* free refill but gave you a couple of free refills before you were charged. So, I saved you money!"

I call BS! Last year, I stayed 47 nights at Hilton hotels. Not one time, during any of those stays, did I get hit with a charge, let alone $4, for a 26-cent refill of syrup and water!

Treating customers like this is called *small thinking*. If the guilty parties are not corrected, it can be an incurable cancer, capable of sinking a business.

This conversation is not about offering deals or getting the rate. Both of those can accompany good *and* bad business operations. Instead, this is a suggestion to reflect on the consistency of your company's outward attitude toward customers regardless of business conditions.

Think about your media outlet. When ratings are high, digital products are delivering and budgets are being made, stressors are down and smiles in-office and to your customers are more plentiful. Smiles are followed by acts of service and an in-general, positive response or attempts to positively satisfy client requests. The small thinking tends to be minimized.

However, when stressors increase, employee to customer request resistance appears—maybe your employees begin selling out of fear, forgetting the importance of service and a smile—and small thinking rears its ugly head.

How can you ensure against small thinking?

Get buy-in to your vision beyond department heads and middle management tiers. Make sure to engage first line of defense, customer interaction roles like AE, production, assistants, and receptionists. Teach them to understand their role as it applies to the vision and importance of positive customer experiences. Empower them to make base level decisions to assist with customer requests. (Think tellers at a bank suggesting a meeting with a manager for a money market upsell to a checking account.)

Discourage the word "no" and make sure the first response is always a form of "yes," with a smile and a pleasant tone, regardless of the client request. As in, "Yes, I'll research that question and get the info back to you" or "Yes, that would be an incredible deal if I could offer that premium commercial to you for that price. Let me locate a few choices more in line with your budget."

Finally, when promoted up or to another media outlet, don't overlook the importance of immediate face-to-face engagement with every single employee to explain and clarify your plan and vision. Failure to do so leaves employees in the dark and less than credible as they resort to small thinking, offending clients with excuses in the process.

WHICH HOTEL CHAIN DOES YOUR TEAM RESEMBLE?

I've spent *a lot of* nights in hotel rooms. In so doing, I've experienced plenty of both the good and bad when it comes to hotel service (as you've just seen in the two previous sections in this chapter).

Judging from the increase in check-in freebies— from free cookies and candy to newspapers and periodicals, and even "to go" snack bags—

competition must be fierce in the service industry.

In recent years, personal messages left in my room from housekeeping seem to have picked up. Some of these notes come complete with a few lifesavers or mint candies. While I appreciate the gesture, I sometimes can't help but wonder if the gesture is a "cover" for a tip request.

If you stay at a Marriott, you'll find they're a bit more blatant in their "tip" requests. Their housekeeping attendants leave an envelope on the nightstand next to a sign that states, "Our caring room attendants enjoyed making your stay warm and comfortable. Please feel free to leave a gratuity to express your appreciation for their efforts."

Disagree if you wish, but I hate being "hit up." As a mature adult, it should be my prerogative whether to match the level of service received with a tip.

While Marriott should be commended for going to bat for their employees, "guilt shaming" guests with a sign and an empty envelope next to the alarm clock feels cheap. It makes one wonder if Marriott is using this "great idea" to increase wages without dipping into the company checkbook.

A stay at Homewood Suites in Huntsville, AL offered hope that not everyone in the hotel industry has gone mad. While unpacking in my room, I discovered what I assumed was another housekeeping note. But this one was different. The letter was inside an envelope, instead of the usual, tri-fold sans envelope. In addition, the envelope was personalized with my name on the outside. Hands down, it was the best "in room" communication I have received to date in my travels.

The letter got straight to the point, welcoming me to the hotel and thanking me for my loyalty to Hilton. It communicated that 100% satisfaction was the expectation. By the way, the positioning of this 100% satisfaction expectation felt much more comfortable than some of the "we must know if you can't give us a perfect score" requests that some car dealers and their service departments employ.

The letter closed with another thank you and a gentle assumptive close, welcoming me back to the hotel in the future. Here's the kicker: the letter was *hand-signed* by the General Manager of the hotel!

Dear Mr. Hannon,

Welcome to the Homewood Suites by Hilton-Huntsville Downtown.

As a Hilton Honors Diamond Member, you are one of our most valuable guests. Thank you for your continued loyalty to Hilton.

Whether you are here for business or pleasure, we hope that you have a wonderful experience while here as our guest. Our award-winning property continues to exceed the expectations of our guests. If you are not 100% satisfied, please do not hesitate to contact myself or the front desk by dialing "0."

Once again, thank you for choosing the Homewood Suites Huntsville Downtown while in Huntsville. We look forward to welcoming you back again in the future.

Sincerely,
Vickie Thrower
General Manager

This was absolute class and the exact positioning that all companies should take with their clients. Take the opportunity to make the moment about the client or guest, not about the business or company. Work with your team to do work that is so good that unprompted compliments from clients become the norm and follow-up business will exceed any small gratuity pool.

Which hotel chain in my story, Marriott or Hilton, gets the prize for making the guest feel appreciated? The answer is pretty obvious.

Does your team resemble Hilton or do your sales stars staple tip envelopes onto client invoices?

A SHORT-TERM LOSS FOR A LONG-TERM GAIN

For many nine-to-fivers, the weekend becomes a time to catch-up and run all the errands that weekday work hours seemingly pre-empt. You know, the fun stuff like getting the car washed, grocery store visits, and laundry pickups. That was the case on no particular Saturday when I set out early on a mission to clear off a list of seven quick stops.

Stop number two on the list was the UPS store

and stop number four was the post office. Doesn't that seem like a waste? I mean, it's just mail, what does it matter who delivers each package and why can't they be in the same store?

Imagine my surprise, upon pulling up to the Sarasota UPS store, and seeing a sign in the window that said, We Also Ship US Mail. "Finally, someone got a clue and decided to make life convenient for us hard-working consumers," I thought to myself.

Carol, at the UPS store counter, noticed my "The Ohio State" golf shirt, and struck up a conversation about the year she and her husband moved the family from the northeast to just outside of Cincinnati, Ohio, long before relocating to Florida. She was an expert at keeping the conversation interesting while simultaneously making sure I was picking the fastest but cheapest options to ship my UPS package. In between sentences, she happily greeted new customers entering the store.

Her tone changed when she got to the final two boxes. "You know, we charge more than the post office would charge you to send these via US Mail. Are you sure you want to send these boxes US Mail from here?" Carol asked. At that point, as though I was being let in on a secret outside the earshot of other customers, Carol resorted to non-verbal communication to answer my follow-up questions, like, "Considerably more?" Her head nod was in the affirmative, before pointing at her watch to show me I could still make the post office before closing.

I whispered, "Thank you so much Carol. I'm really taken back by your honesty." She responded, "It's those good midwestern values." Maybe so, but I think it really has more to do with Carol's attitude, her understanding of business, and her heart of service.

Some of you reading this may disagree with Carol. Maybe you think it wasn't right that her suggestion cost the UPS Store owner a few bucks. I get it. However, the bigger picture is really a short-term loss for a long-term gain.

Before writing this story, I explained this experience to probably a dozen Sarasota residents or more, many of whom will remember my story and will drive cross-town, passing up three other UPS Stores to see Carol at the Bee Ridge Road location. The next time I need to ship UPS, what store do you think I'll visit?

Carol gave up about twelve dollars in the short-term but is sure to get many hundreds for the shipping store, long-term.

The question for you is, do you have a team full of Carols, or do you have a team that pushes their own agenda to close deals and opportunities that may not fit, or may not be in the best interest of the client?

With today's corporate sales pressure, maybe there's a bigger question. How are you managing your team's effort at achieving revenue success in each of your multiple channels, products, and digital opportunities? Are your sellers looking out for the client? A quick investigation of your churn, or non-returning clients, is a great place to start answering that question.

PUT OUT THE FIRE BEFORE IT STARTS

Upon hearing the emergency audio tone, the airline flight attendant stopped serving drinks rather abruptly and headed for the nearest on-plane phone to confer with the pilot.

Oil was spewing from the blown right-side engine and we were going to make an emergency landing in Memphis.

This particular evening, I was headed halfway across the country to a state broadcasting association convention, where hundreds of media stars were told "yours truly" would be speaking at 1030am sharp the next morning. In these types of (thankfully few) instances, I immediately go into backup planning mode, checking alternative flights and even rental car availability, in case an all-night drive is the only on-time arrival option.

No backup plan was necessary, as Delta was quick to dispatch a plane from Cincinnati to pick up our group of stranded passengers in Memphis. The biggest inconvenience was landing at our destination three and a half hours after our original itinerary. But, the bonus was the extended break in Memphis, allowing for enough time to enjoy a delicious BBQ sandwich, one which few cities can rival.

So, this whole incident was really a blip on my travel radar. It was really nothing to get upset over. That's why I was surprised when Delta Airlines took the situation much more seriously than I did. They were extremely quick to turn a possible "thorn into a rose" with an apology email and free bonus miles. Delta sent this email before our plane landed. Here's the email in its entirety:

From: Delta Air Lines
Subject: Delta Air Lines, Customer Care

Hello John,

RE: Case Number 24247...

I'm sure it may have been unsettling when Flight 3516, operated by Endeavor Airlines as Delta Connection, had to make an unscheduled landing this evening into Memphis due to a mechanical issue with the airplane. The crew followed established procedures to ensure your safety and land uneventfully. As a result, another aircraft was made available so that we could continue the flight to Springfield. I know it was important to get you to your destination on-time and I'm very sorry for any inconvenience this caused.

We Appreciate Your Business

As a goodwill gesture, I've deposited 5,000 bonus miles into your account. Please allow three business days for the mileage to be posted.

Thanks for Flying Delta

We look forward to seeing you on another Delta flight.

Regards,

Heidi Gould
General Manager
Customer Care

My hope is that this personal story resonates with you the next time an advertising client registers a complaint with your media outlet. Don't be tempted to judge if the issue is big or small. Trust me, if someone is motivated enough to contact you, then the issue looms large in their eyes.

To preserve their loyalty, you need to respond to their complaint as soon as is absolutely possible. If the situation is going to take some investigation, then respond accordingly, thanking them for their concern and patience.

In your final response to their complaint, "wow"

them with kindness, offer a freebie as a gesture of goodwill, let them know how much you sincerely appreciate their business, and finally, thank them for their future confidence in your organization. Doing so will put out the proverbial "fire before it starts" and, as a result, will secure your client's continuing loyalty.

SERVICE LETTER MISTAKES I HOPE YOUR SELLERS AREN'T MAKING

Many companies follow up with, "How did we do?" service letters. Because of my heavy travel schedule, between airlines, hotels, rental and car services, I average a couple dozen or more of these service letters a month.

The requests in these communications are getting more aggressive and, quite frankly, I sometimes scratch my head, wondering if anyone even bothers to proofread anymore.

The most recent unbelievable example is below. The hotel chain is listed but the name and phone number of the sender has been changed to protect the guilty.

From: DG Assistant General Manager
To: john@jimdoyle.com

Subject: Your current stay at the Hilton Garden Inn
Greetings from the Hilton Garden Inn!

I want to take this opportunity to say thanks for

140

staying at my hotel. We believe your entire stay should be nothing less than a "10" experience. My goal is to ensure we deliver service that exceeds expectations to each and every guest before they leave. If you are to receive a survey from us, and feel you would not be able to rate us a "10" I would like to know. Please share with me any reasons about this stay that we should discuss, I promise to do whatever it takes to ensure satisfaction. If you already feel as if we are a "10", I would still love to hear what one thing we could do to enhance your stay. It's our Count On Me. Guaranteed.

Thanks again for staying with us and I look forward to any feedback! Please do not hesitate to contact me at (555) 555-5555 or simply reply to this e-mail to reach me.

We look forward to you returning please visit <u>www.hiltongardeninn.com</u> to book a reservation at our hotel.

Hospitably,
Assistant General Manager

Grammatical errors aside, what is the first thing you notice when reading this letter? Isn't it extremely one-sided? There are 22 references to "I, my, we, us" and "our," vs. 6 "you" references. Given that information, who is this letter about?

One doesn't have to be psychic to determine this Assistant General Manager has a financial bonus tied to guest service ratings. But, to be honest, I may have respected this manager more if they had skipped the poor attempt at sincerity and written something like, "Anything less than a 10 means less money in my paycheck, so please forgive any unpleasant experiences when filling out the survey form."

I'm going to take the high road here and assume that the author of this follow-up service email "doesn't know what they don't know." Ultimately, who is responsible for teaching and making sure gaffes like this don't land in customers' inboxes? You guessed it—this individual's manager.

Time for a gut check. As a manager and leader, are you confident that every single individual on your team is professional and error free in their written follow-up?

Here's a sales meeting idea. Have everyone on your team bring their last half-dozen written client communications. Start the meeting by circulating the above hotel email. Open up the floor for disbelief comments, discussion, and correction steps. Then, have your sellers review the communications they brought to the meeting. I'm guessing they will now understand the importance and need for crafting a professional and proper message when following up with clients and prospects.

THE FAST BEAT THE SLOW

One or my favorite quotes, describing today's business environment, comes from the founder of the FOX Television Network, Rupert Murdoch. He stated, "The world is changing very fast. Big will not beat small anymore; it will be the fast beating the slow."

Recently, I experienced this "speed" from a cosmetic dentist returning my inquiry via her website. She was one of three dentists that I contacted and was by far the smallest of the three offices. In the below exchange you can see that the doctor personally responded to my question—in just 22 minutes! Did I mention this was on a Sunday?!

On Apr 29, at 5:44 PM, John Hannon wrote:

Have 2 front teeth with small cracks and am concerned their repair will not hold. Would like a free consultation to discuss my options, pricing, and to learn about your experience with these situations. Thank you. John Hannon

From: *Chris (Dr. K)*
Sent: *Sunday, April 29, 6:06 PM*
Subject: *Re: Contact from Website*

Good evening John,

I am on a long drive back to Florida and just received your email to our website. Thought I had the time to respond personally! I would be very pleased to discuss what your options might be. Your situation is what we deal with on a daily basis. It is truly my passion.

Our albums of smile enhancements have been completed for your viewing, which gives you the opportunity to see if our office and care are a good fit for you.

Becky will call you tomorrow for your complimentary consultation.

Looking forward to meeting you.

Christine K. DMD
Sent from my iPhone

Of the three dentists I contacted, can you guess which one got my business?

The second dentist got back to me four days after my inquiry; and the third dentist took over a week. The timing of responses from dentist two and three really didn't matter. I had already been to see Dr. K and she'd won my business, thanks to her speedy and attentive reply.

While serving as President for Jim Doyle & Associates, I was fortunate to work with a few TV stations that were shining examples of the fast beating the slow. These stations weren't part of large, consolidated many-station groups. They were typically owned by small broadcasters, many with a portfolio of only a few stations.

The sales stars at these properties were in friendly competition with their peers around the conference room table, draining ink pens when we'd discuss market advertising opportunities. When the meeting was over, one could witness the speed with which these sellers exited the room, as they wanted to be the first to claim each new business prospect. They didn't cry about their small group size or their lack of tools or ratings, despite the fact that a heavily fortified, "large group" station competitor was likely just down the street. They enjoyed "first in" leverage, rarely running into a client who'd say, "Your competitor told me..." Why? Because, as Rupert Murdoch said, "...it will be the fast beating the slow."

SOMETIMES, BEST INTENTIONS FALL SHORT

Once a week, sometimes twice if I'm being truthful, my car makes an office route detour to the local Starbucks. I've never really been a huge coffee fan but have developed an affinity for a hot caramel drink loaded with sugar and whipped cream.

Recently, I was on the receiving end of a bitter, dark chocolate, concoction that was a 180-degree opposite of the delicious caramel drink my taste buds were anticipating. Realizing that the barista had delivered the wrong drink, I circled the building and headed back through the drive-thru.

Starbucks has not built raving loyalty by being

a place to *buy* a cup of coffee. Instead, they're a place to *experience* a cup of coffee—where the focus is on the customer. Their store atmosphere, product consistency, and employee training are all in support of providing a superior experience for every single Starbucks shopper.

That's why, upon explaining the drink mistake to barista Seth, his smile, sincere apology, and immediate statement to "...fix a new, correct, what you ordered drink" was not a surprise. However, it was a surprise when the new, correct, coffee drink was accompanied with a gift card. Seth apologized for the mistake again, and followed up with, "Please take this gift card for a free drink on me your next visit." Wow, talk about over-the-top treatment... that is until getting to the office and reading the gift card!

To be clear, I had no plan to squeeze the coffee giant out of a free cup of joe. I simply wanted the correct drink, maybe a tiny, "We're sorry" and a sincere, "Have a great day!" There was absolutely no thought of "free," gift card or otherwise, when pulling up to the drive-thru for a remake. Seth took it upon himself to create a Starbucks "wow" by throwing in a gift card. But Seth screwed up. You see, the cost of the caramel coffee is nearly *five* dollars. The value of the gift card Seth comped was only $2.50, or 50% of full value. Unbeknownst to Seth, he *had not* given me a free drink, but instead the equivalent of a half-off coupon. His effort fell short of the expectation.

Am I upset? No. Will I ever go to Starbucks again? Yes. Will I call the customer service hotline and demand they comp another $2.50? Of course not!

The point of the story has zero to do with the lost opportunity of an additional $2.50.

Sometimes, in one's best effort to please—to make a positive out of a potential negative—the well-meaning best intentions fall short, and unfortunately, in many instances the "giver" doesn't even realize their mistake.

Except for professional scammers, most customers and business clients would be satisfied with a store, company or business representative owning up to their mistake, making it good, and sincerely apologizing. However, as barista Seth needs to learn, when an attempt is made to replace a mistake with a customer "wow," the offer should not only meet, but preferably exceed, customer expectations.

Turning thorns into roses, no matter how small the issue, is key to collecting raving fans and creating long-term customer loyalty.

UNDERSTANDING A CLIENT'S FEAR OF ECONOMIC UNCERTAINTY

On a near daily basis, Jim Doyle & Associates would receive marketing questions on various categories.

Even during times when employment was at record numbers, with lots of dollars being pumped into the economy, we would often get questions dealing with economic uncertainty. Below is one of my responses on this topic.

Question: *Hey John, could you give me some feedback on current economic conditions? What do you think business owners want to hear/learn about? What are the economic topics that would make potential clients stop and listen and to feel better about continuing their advertising?*
Sincerely, Tim

Answer: *Dear Tim, we teach 3 phases of client optimism:*

*1. **Growth** (client is excited about the future, likely to take more risk.)*

*2. **Fear** (client is concerned about the unknown, possible down turns, "doom and gloom" headlines.)*

*3. **Don't Rock The Boat** (client listens with one ear, they know everything, unlikely they will be sold unless you can help them connect the dots as though they came up with the solution on their own.)*

The easiest sale is Fear. This goes all the way back to 1940's insurance sales and the training that encouraged questions like, "Don't you have an obligation to ensure your family is not destitute in the event of your untimely death?"

Establishing fear through specific lines of questioning is the quickest way to get noticed in this cluttered space. The descriptions should make one feel the fear of loss. Maybe a loss of something they take for granted now that they never thought about being without. It's easy to make that connection to loss of money. (Sure, you're set now, but how many weeks could you survive without a paycheck?)

All indicators predict loan interest rate increases. Mortgage rates will follow, forcing higher house prices and making some purchases difficult for first-time and low saver buyers. As housing sales slip, home repair and remodeling businesses will be pushed into the black, as they accommodate those who choose to remodel and wait out the rates. Home and apartment rentals will increase.

The same scenario will happen with car sales. People will hold onto cars longer, which will force manufacturers to offer incentives to trim the bloat of inventory. Expect a spike in lease sales. Finally, used car prices will increase, thanks to demand as lot inventories suffer.

Credit card debt will increase, which is an upside for consolidation companies. Bankruptcy claims will increase, bringing business to attorneys.

The key here is how does one navigate the day-to-day economic shifts, while still ensuring income during retirement; while at the same time ensuring they have enough to last the entirety of living? Also, how does one get on the positive cash side of the equation so that money is working for the individual instead of the individual working for money? (For example, buy rental properties at lower interest rates for the equity and in perpetuity rental income.)

It's an interesting study how a single economic indicator can tip other influences as easily as a line of toppling dominos. The upside? History provides a bit of reliable guidance when advising advertisers who may be too cautious and reluctant to continue marketing their businesses. The worst thing an advertiser can do during windows of economic uncertainty is nothing!

A GREAT COMMERCIAL SELLS PRODUCT

When I fell off a ladder in the beginning of 2019, severely breaking my right leg in four places, the surgeon was generous with the metal. He utilized *nine* screws and *two* plates to get me back to kicking field goals in record time.

There's only so much one can do when restricted to a no-weight-bearing, no-walking, 12-week recovery. The days consist of being chained to a chair, reading, writing, making phone calls and answering emails, between the obligatory recovery naps, all while the TV hums in the background. It was peaceful in the beginning. But after a while, cabin fever strikes and the only lifeline to the outside world consistently casts a blue hue and sound from the wall across the room. By the end of the first few weeks of this schedule, I arrived at a conclusion about our business. It's not really a secret, but it is likely discussed in whispers in the dark hallways of your offices because no one wants to upset a "paying" client.

As an industry, our local client commercials are terrible.

Please don't misunderstand—the production values of some of the commercials are incredible. They're high-def, hollywoodesque, entertaining award winners. It's apparent that the creators and producers of these commercials are talented, and they probably have a shelf full of local Emmy and Addy trophies in support of their expertise.

However, a trophy-winning commercial isn't necessarily a great commercial for the client. A commercial that sells product and makes the cash register ring is a great commercial. It should be singular in delivery, feature the client's "one thing," and have a clear call-to-action. Short of these components, a commercial is not effective if it *does not* move product. Pat Norris, Senior Vice President of Jim Doyle & Associates, describes this situation as the "ninety-day cancellation plan," and it's likely the reason your AE's become frustrated over the objection, "I tried TV and it didn't work."

The insanity is that your sellers can do everything by the book during the sales process, but then something gets lost in translation when the AE transitions the client to the creative team for commercial production. Worse yet, an agency provides another "award winning," non-selling commercial for the campaign. Or, maybe the client insists on putting her kids, grandkids, dog, and neighbor in the commercial, leaving little "selling" time for their product. Then, ninety days later comes the cancellation.

Encourage your team to take ownership of the creative process and to make sure the necessary "selling" components are included in the finished copy and not on the edit room floor.

Help them understand that a commercial that sells product(s) for the client, and in turn secures a client's advertising renewal, trumps a trophy every day of the week!

WELCOME TO LARRY'S BATHROOM

As a road warrior, I averaged just under 300,000 flight miles annually. With that kind of travel schedule, one would think that I have seen everything there is to see in an airport. That was pretty much my thinking until one Tuesday night when I stopped at a Terminal C restroom between flights in Atlanta.

"Welcome to Larry's bathroom!" the short, slightly round, leaning-against-the-wall janitor proudly exclaimed. Never having witnessed this kind of public bathroom welcome, I was understandably surprised.

Out of the corner of my eye, I watched in amazement as Larry jumped to activate the auto soap dispensers and pull paper towels for the travelers making their way to the sinks. All the while, Larry continued talking... in rhymes. "This is Larry's bathroom. The place to be when you gotta' pee. If you're in a rush, no need to flush."

At this point, the bathroom "customers" were bent over in shared laughter. But Larry wasn't done, "For you gentlemen in the stalls, it has been said that all good things come to an end. Here's hoping good things come out of your end!"

Here's where the story takes an unexpected turn. Everyone in the restroom tried to hand various denominations of money to Larry upon their exit. He refused all gestures.

I told him he deserved the cash for providing everyone a few laughs and asked why he wouldn't take the money. He responded, "No, I'm just doing my job."

Wow. This is a janitor, tasked with cleaning up some of the vilest of messes imaginable, who still finds it in his heart to add fun to each traveler's day with absolutely no expectations in return, and he calls that, "...just doing my job."

Take stock of your team for a moment. Can you identify the Larrys? If not, maybe it's time for an honest assessment of your environment. What is your current culture and what is it going to take to creature the culture that you not only want, but need?

WHO HAS THE POWER?

Always be aware of who has the power in negotiation.

If you're buying a car, you may have more power on the last day of the month vs. the fourth or fifth day of the month, when you may experience a lack of power. Car dealers want to make a deal. They want to have a bigger month and only have so many days in the month to "sell" and hit their numbers.

Many years ago, as an up-and-coming account executive, I would often run into clients who advertised with the market boomer, despite the fact that they hated writing a check to the station every month. The sellers and managers at the station had a reputation for being a bit egotistical, and rarely, if ever, came off their perceived inflated prices. As a result, many clients didn't necessarily like dealing with the station, but the station's bloated ratings cushioned the return on investment risk that accompanied advertising on a competitor.

Over time, the boomer's ratings began to erode, and clients started moving their money. The sellers and managers at the station had to swallow a lot of pride, as they faced an uphill battle in trying to repair years of relationship apathy. The irony is that this headache could have been avoided had the station considered the possibility that the pendulum of power could, and usually does, shift.

I love the line that says, "Figure out who has the power, but then act like you have none." Even if I have a tremendous amount of power in a negotiation, I'm not going to be arrogant. Please heed my warning. For the most part, the client knows that when you have leverage, you don't have to rub it in because they will make you pay down the line when circumstance shift the power back in their favor. Arrogance damages you, the relationship, and the potential sale.

So, figure out who has the power in the negotiation. If it's you, act like you have none. Strive for a win-win negotiation to leave the client feeling that they are working with a professional.

THE BENEFITS OF A BRAINSTORM

One of the most effective ways to build long-term client relationships is to differentiate yourself or become known for things the competition is *not* doing.

My favorite differentiator is a station brainstorm. By hosting a brainstorm, you create intimate networking opportunities that build business relationships among clients.

A lot of business owners experience the same issues and have the same problems regardless of their category of business. To help them, why not host a client brainstorm? Invite different clients, who have like ideas and issues, to your office. Then bring them into a large room or studio, where you'll also include station personnel, like your promotions department, creative services, sales, and various other department head managers. Fill the room with white boards and easel tablets, ready to capture the discussions of the issues that those businesses are facing. Each business owner is encouraged to offer input into the others' situations. How much is shared is up to the business owners. But, to ensure there's a positive air, it's important not to invite competitors to the same brainstorm.

When the businesses leave, three things will happen: They're going to understand that the whole station is behind them, not just their account executive. They're also going to make some new contacts and will recognize that your outlet was the conduit for the contacts. Thirdly, because you're going to solve some of their problems, they'll be extremely thankful, maybe even pleasantly surprised, that you've taken a special interest in their business and given of your resources freely—something your competitors are likely not doing!

CHAPTER 6

FOCUS ON YOUR CAREER

*Choose a job you love, and you will never
have to work a day in your life.*

-Confucius

YOUR NEW BOSS IS A TV OUTSIDER

As consolidation of companies welcomes C-suite
bean counters, and not necessarily the passionate
broadcasters who used to dominate our board
rooms, I've run into more than a few general
managers who are frustrated that their new
corporate bosses have no television industry
experience and, as a result, don't understand the
business.

Outsiders in the form of "specialists" are
responsible for guiding, directing, and negotiating
our performance to an acceptable "street" number.
Want to know why your new COO was hired away
from a legal firm and not a competing TV group?
Because retransmission compensation has moved

from the bonus column to the necessary column of cash flow sheets, and the individual responsible for maximizing and negotiating the comp had better be a contract legal expert. So, in many ways, welcoming these corporate newbies to our companies isn't a bad thing—except when it comes to a passion for the medium.

If you're a broadcast purist—the kind of individual who started in radio as a teen and never looked back—what can you do if you suddenly find yourself reporting to a boss hired freshly from anywhere *but* television?

First, don't assume. Don't assume that just because their résumé doesn't indicate media experience that they lack the skill set to be a leader in our medium. They have obviously displayed leadership in another field, or they wouldn't have been tapped to be your boss.

Next, volunteer. Volunteer to be a "go to" resource for the transition into the TV world. Make yourself available for "why?" and "how do we...?" questions. During their visits, provide opportunities for sales call ride-alongs, tower and transmitter tours, behind camera seats during newcasts, participation in department meetings, local upfront "new season" launch parties; in general, anything and everything that gets one excited to learn more about our business. You may be thinking, "Yeah, right, and open myself up to scrutiny?" If that's a concern, then skip this step. However, if I were you, I would consider this an opportunity to seed a relationship and to shine a spotlight on your team's performance highlights.

Lastly, keep an open mind. Be willing to take input, and as tough as it may be, ask for input. Sometimes a comment from a set of inexperienced industry eyes is the spark that is needed to establish improved ways of operation or increased levels of output.

BUYING THEIR OWN TOOLS IS THE PRICE OF ADMISSION FOR EMPLOYMENT

My speaking and training schedule with Jim Doyle & Associates sometimes included time in front of audiences and partner stations in the heart of the Louisiana/Texas gas and oil belts. After the obligatory Atlanta plane connection, I would typically board a regional puddle-jumper and fight for elbow space with a crowd of, what I was convinced, were the toughest blue-collar workers punching a time clock.

Most were very friendly and not averse to a conversation with a stranger to pass the flight time. The majority of these fuel field workers, whether female or male, traveled in work boots, had callused hands, and were employed to do everything from operating drill machinery to welding towers to driving water buffaloes that sprinkle ground water in an effort to minimize the dust that's known to kick up during full plant operation.

There was one similarity that struck me as interesting. To an individual, every one of these employees traveled with a hard hat. There were also many who wore belts with slots for various radios and electronics, and nearly all placed tool belts or tool boxes filled with things like wrenches, screwdrivers, hammers, nut drivers, pliers, welding masks, and heavy-duty work gloves in the plane's overhead storage.

After noticing this on the first couple of flights, my curiosity got the better of me and I had to ask, "Wouldn't it be easier to leave the tools at the job site instead of packing and repacking them for travel every couple of weeks?" With a confused look, my seatmate responded, "No, we have to buy our tools and they're expensive. I don't trust anyone else to use them, so it's no big deal to carry them back and forth."

Wow. Before even being hired, he had to purchase his own tools. That's the expectation in his industry (and the same I've found for others, like construction.)

This scenario made me think of the thousands of media AE's and managers in our business. At every single media operation I've visited, there were two types of sellers: 1) those who would make an investment in themselves and their careers; and 2) those who exclusively relied on their company to seek out and pay for everything.

The individuals committed to personal development are the first at an event to approach and want book recommendations. They want to know where I got the portable speaker that pumps the sound out of my laptop or the website address and the monthly subscription for the latest video email software. They will spend their "outside of work" hours listening to industry audio instruction or reading books like *Engaged Management* that they purchased on their own— and didn't expense.

In contrast, the individuals who expect the company to pay for everything, tend to *only* invest time for self-improvement "during work hours." Some, despite being six-digit earners, may expect the company to pay for things like Rotary, Chamber, the local tip club or JDA's The Leaders Edge membership!

No doubt you were already aware of these differences, but have you ever considered the question, "Which number, 1 or 2, is generally the better performer?" I pick number 1. It's not proven yet by business research, and certainly there are exceptions, but my gut says if one has skin in the game and is willing to invest in themselves, then they will ultimately be the more successful.

Then, there are those in careers, like my new gas and oil field friends who don't blink an eye paying for an assortment of expensive tools. It's the price of admission for employment. Maybe that's why the media people who are hesitant to invest in themselves aren't fuel field workers!

CHANGE YOUR PERSPECTIVE

The National Association of Broadcasters Small Market Television Exchange is my favorite industry show of the year. Some of the best money-making ideas and creative approaches to selling digital and TV products are revealed here.

The year 2018 marked my fourteenth year going to this event. So, after attending for many years, one can understand why the NAB SMTE is a bit of an annual reunion for me. Funny though, despite the affair annually rotating from coast to coast among various cities, my office had never been close enough to drive. In fact, I'd flown to every NAB SMTE that I'd attended, that is until Nashville in 2018.

That year, I decided to ride a motorcycle from my home in Sarasota, Florida to the show in Nashville, Tennessee. Actually, two Jim Doyle & Associates business partners and fellow motorcycle riders, Tom Ray and Pat Norris, had decided, many months prior, that they would join me on the ride. However, post-NAB travel obligations required them to fly, meaning both had to leave their steel horses behind. Thus, a *Three Amigos* trip turned into a solo journey.

Round trip, the adventure set me back *four* travel days, through *four* states, *five* rainstorms, and over 1,555 miles of incredible American scenery. I'd do it again in a heartbeat. Why? Am I crazy? Maybe, but for me this trip was really about achieving a different perspective.

When one is inside their own head for over 1,500 miles, lots of problems get solved and questions get answered. The "why's" and "why not's" gain clarity, and priorities get rearranged. Upon completion of the trip, my body was physically tired, but my mind was on full alert—all thanks to breaking my plane flight habit and being open to being in the moment and taking in a new environment.

Many of you may be thinking, "Good for you, John. But I don't have a motorcycle, nor do I have a week to get inside my own head!"

I get it. To be fair, a motorcycle trip isn't for everyone. However, you can experience perspective changes by shaking up your daily habits. Because we're creatures of habit, this exercise can be difficult. But after a while, locating these opportunities for change become fun. Here are some thoughts to get you started:

Opportunities For A Change Of Perspective

- Set the alarm 45 minutes earlier one day and hit the gym, walk the dog, read a fun book or sit outside and observe the sun coming up.
- One day, avoid the temptation to check your email when you wake up.
- Write a quote for your kids' lunch box.
- Take your kids, wife, husband, spouse, partner or friend to breakfast before work.
- Instead of drinking coffee, try tea or a cold drink to start your day.
- Go ahead, eat the leftover cake for breakfast. After all, what are doughnuts?
- If you normally eat out at lunch, pack a lunch for yourself.
- Try wearing that crazy, but professional tie, that you never wear but for some reason can't let go of.
- If your office is close enough, try riding your bike or walking to work.
- For an enjoyable change of scenery, drive a different route to the office—one that you've rarely or never driven before.
- Listen to a different talk/morning show or music that your kids listen to or music you have never heard during your drive.
- If you park in the same space daily, try parking across the lot in a different space.

- Sit in a different chair or spot, or try standing during your morning meeting.

- Enter your building through a different door that forces you to take a different hallway route to your office. That's a lot of "good mornings" to different faces.

- Throw out your To-Do list and schedule everything you need to accomplish as appointments on your calendar. You'll be amazed at how unimportant some things are that currently get moved to the next day's To-Do list.

- Meet your kids, wife, husband, spouse, partner or friend for a workday picnic lunch. Why should this only be reserved for weekends?

- Leave work early and surprise the family for no reason.

- Eat dessert before starting on your meal.

- One night, after dinner, shoot hoops, pass a ball or frisbee, go for a short bike ride, play video games—anything to break up the evening. Don't worry, the DVR will record your favorite shows for viewing later.

- Speaking of late viewing, stay up really late binge-watching a new series or that new show you were thinking of watching "one day." Do it on a weeknight and don't worry about how early you have to get up the next day!

The whole point is to substitute different things, environments, and ways of doing things in place of the habits that we've come to accept. There is certainly nothing wrong with our daily habits, and in some ways, many of them are positive influences on our lives, for example, daily exercise. However, it would seem if one did the exact same exercise, at the same time every day, for the exact same duration, that exercise and the thoughts toward exercise would get pretty boring.

My encouragement to you is to invigorate your mind by changing your perspective. Be bold and don't be afraid, on occasion, to separate from your habits or your comfort level.

If doing so is too uncomfortable, you can always go back to your old habits the next day!

IT'S OK IF YOU DON'T WANT TO GO TO WORK TODAY

The day was a wall-to-wall packed, 17-hour day, filled with webinars, phone calls, office meetings and presentation prep, all while focusing at least one eye on multiple device screens. Suffice it to say, I was mentally and physically drained by the time my head hit the pillow, well past midnight.

There's a sports saying, "Leave it all on the field." That day, as it relates to business, yes, I had left it all on the field. As you have probably experienced, there is satisfaction to that feeling.

But, there can also be a downside. Sometimes, when hours increase and unpleasant tasks fill our schedules, the fun seems to disappear and our lack of enthusiasm infects the air and culture of our organizations. It is in these moments when the voice in your head gains volume, attempting to convince you that you no longer like your job or those people in the office or those clients who call you with complaints.

Does it surprise you to hear me say, "That's OK?"

Hey, you're human, so of course negative thoughts are going to surface from time to time. The cause for concern and career choice reflection is when the number of days with negative thoughts outweigh the number of days with positive thoughts.

So, what should you do to motivate a positive attitude change on the days you just don't feel like going to the office? You could take an impromptu vacation day. Admittedly, doing this doesn't seem to work for me. My mind doesn't let go of work commitments that had to be cleared to take the unscheduled day off!

The best solution is to shake up your normal ritual and break away from your daily habits. Set the alarm a bit earlier. Make breakfast for the family. Get in some physical activity like a short bike ride or walking the dog. Read. Go to the office before the team arrives for some productive quiet time. Schedule lunch with a close friend. Telephone a mentor. Review your "hooray me" file—your collection of congratulatory notes, messages, and thanks from those who have appreciated your work. Then, share your positive lift by *engaging* co-workers in the hallways, sincerely taking an interest in non-work-related topics.

Lastly, commit yourself to making sure that *today will not be like yesterday.* Of course, you'll be productive, however, instead of filling your time plowing through paperwork and undesirable tasks, make certain to concentrate your efforts on the priorities and things that continue to satisfy the passions that drew you into this industry in the first place.

MAKE TODAY YOUR ONE DAY

"One day, I will..."

Have you ever heard someone say that? Maybe, you have made that statement?

"One day, I will... buy a Porsche, write a book, lose 30 pounds, vacation in Bora Bora, become a Vice President, lead a team that makes every single annual revenue budget, etc."

It doesn't matter how the sentence ends. What matters is one's ability to *act* on the statement or goal.

Many individuals are great at writing down their S.M.A.R.T. goals: Specific, Measurable, Achievable, Realistic, and Time-bound. But, without an action

170

plan to achieve those goals, individuals become *dreamers* as opposed to *doers*. The "doers" are the winners in life because they are not only committed to their SMART goals, they also have a multi-step plan of action and accountability for achieving each goal. The absolute best in this crowd of doers can tell you, in great detail, where they are in the process of exceeding their objectives.

Note that I said, "...where they are in the process..." Concentrating on your commitment—the time spent working to advance you toward goal fulfillment—is the key to accomplishing more than you ever thought possible.

Most failure is the result of not investing enough time to make the goal happen. For the best opportunity at success, you need to develop the habit of literally scheduling appointments on your calendar to spend time working toward each goal. Doing so will allow you to track your progress by any measure of day, week, month or even longer. You will be able to quickly determine if your time invested is enough to reach your target.

For example, as part of your aggressive recruiting plan, maybe you have stated, "One day, I will have had a discussion with each of the top 10 advertising sellers in the market." How many attempts at contact with these sellers did you make last week? Or, have you invited any of them to meet for coffee in the next month? You have to be honest in your personal accountability. If the answer is zero, what outcome can you expect? A goal without an action plan is simply a dream that becomes the subject of, "One day, I will..." Become a doer. Make today your "one day" to take action to transform your dreams into a reality of accomplishments.

PRACTICE MAKES PERFECT

I remember *three* well-respected, successful, sales managers telling me, in the same week, that their sellers were trained on "that" (pick any topic) a few years ago. Each continued to explain to me how it would be a waste of time to visit the content with their sellers again. The irony is that one of the sales teams had experienced a 50% turnover rate in two years, so half the team hadn't even participated in the last training session!

I don't think any less of a manager when I hear this response, unless they refuse to consider their "one and done" thinking might not be the best course of action for a successful and profitable sales culture.

Success in business is derived from repetition and consistency. Don't believe me? According to the American Society For Training Development (ASTD), companies that invest in training enjoy a 24% higher profit margin than those that don't. Further, individuals are more engaged and tend to stay longer at companies that invest in educating employees.

It's the same in life. Have you ever heard of an Olympic hopeful sprinter who trains by running really fast around the quarter mile track at the local high school... once?! Or, how about a Major League Baseball designated hitter who never takes batting practice or a pitcher who never warms up before going on the mound?

It simply doesn't happen. It's the same reason some of us go to mass or church every Sunday because we need to be reminded of what, and how, to incorporate and do the right things.

But, simply hearing the content over and over is not good enough.

The more one puts into action the knowledge from the lessons learned, the better the performance will be. However, the work is never ending. It's called "practice."

The most successful managers believe that "practice makes perfect." As a result, these leaders place a premium on opportunities that encourage their sellers to learn, improve, and sharpen their skill sets.

REVENUE SOLVES ALL ISSUES

In your TV management role, what is your #1 priority?

When I ask this question of TV GM's, responses

vary from, "To build news ratings" or "To be visible in the market" or even some form of "Management and motivation of personnel."

To be sure, many of those responses are important, at least to the individual. The managers answering that question are passionate about their role and prove such by dedicating their time and effort to what they perceive to be the priority. However, I would contend that things like news ratings, market visibility, and motivating personnel are *not* priorities. They are simply steps to achieving the *ultimate* priority.

So, allow me to pose the question again. In your TV management role, what is your #1 priority?

The answer is... revenue.

Ask any C-suite executive—many of whom are your bosses—the same question and they will likely respond with "revenue" in unison.

Yes, all of the day-to-day actions are important, and many are likely high priorities on your to-do list, but they are all in support of increasing the financial bottom-line.

Don't believe me? How uncomfortable is the conversation with your bosses if the sales audit reveals your ratings went up 16% but your total revenue share dropped 10%?

Reverse the scenario. Let's say ratings were down 10% but your revenue share increased by 16%. From experience, I can confirm the corporate conversation is much friendlier in this example. Why? Because revenue solves all issues.

Keep that in mind the next time you're consumed with things that are really just "tasks" on your way to building the #1 priority.

SCIENCE CAUTIONS WORKAHOLICS

How many hours a week do you work? Forty? Fifty? Sixty? More?

Are your long work hours a bragging point; a badge of career success? Does it make you feel as though you've accomplished something; that you're setting the right example for the team by being the first car in the parking lot and the last to leave?

If so, we've had something in common... until a few years ago.

I'd been burning the candle at both ends. A book release, an unforgiving travel schedule, and intense prep for additional speaking dates left little time to handle the day-to-day business of running a company. It was only natural then, to increase work hours in order to catch up. Like many of you, my business background is rooted in the belief that "hours equal productivity." But for some reason, the additional hours didn't result in catching up. In fact, it was almost as if those additional hours were unproductive.

Don't believe it? I didn't either until reading an article from Tom Papamoronis, a columnist for *Inc.*

Magazine. The title, "Science Says You Shouldn't Work More Than This Number Of Hours Per Week" (May 2016), really grabbed me, as I'm one who needs the credibility of proven research, not conjecture.

Tom Papamoronis wrote that science has determined working too much can negatively impact your productivity and can be hazardous to your health. Additionally:

- Little productive work occurs after 50 hours per week
- Working more than 10 hours a day is associated with a 60 percent jump in risk of cardiovascular issues.
- 10 percent of those working 50 to 60 hours report relationship problems; the rate increases to 30 percent for those working more than 60 hours.
- Working more than 40 hours a week is associated with increased alcohol and tobacco consumption, as well as unhealthy weight gain in men and depression in women.
- In white collar jobs, productivity declines by as much as 25 percent when workers put in 60 or more weekly hours.
- Many of the "workaholic" problems tie to stress, which connect to hormonal imbalances. Specifically, stress raises

cortisol, which can disrupt sleep, appetite, blood pressure, immune system function, memory/cognition, mood, and more.

I know what some of you are thinking. It's these kinds of studies that substantiate lazy work forces. It encourages clock-watching instead of project progress. After all, builders of companies and top business leaders didn't get there by counting work hours to stay in their maximum productivity zone. I agree, but I've also come around to the thought that fifty-, sixty-, or seventy-hour or more work weeks should be the exception, not the norm.

Running a work treadmill that never stops is not good for your mental or physical well-being and a less-than-optimum you is not good for your business or your relationships.

WHEN WE NEEDED YOU THE MOST, YOU GAVE US YOUR VERY BEST

When Urban Meyer retired as The Ohio State University head football coach, it was not only the end of an era at The Ohio State, but also the end of an incredible coaching career; one of the best in the history of college football. Haters are going to hate, but numbers don't lie. Meyer spent 17 seasons as a head coach at 4 different colleges, compiling a .854-win percentage and capturing 3 National Championship titles.

After his final game as a coach, a 28-23 Rose

Bowl win over Washington State, on-field reporters jockeyed for position to capture Meyer summarizing his coaching career. As many great leaders do, Urban spent little time discussing himself, and set about heaping praise on his family, for understanding and supporting the sacrifices necessary to pursue success. Next, he profusely thanked the many mentors, coaches, and individuals who had made such a positive impact on his career. His final thanks was reserved for all the players who comprised the winning teams that made his coaching career so successful. He was proud that his players subscribed to team over self and, when necessary, came together to fight adversity.

Meyer closed his player appreciation by mentioning a mantra painted on a wall of The Ohio State football facility, *"When we needed you the most, you gave us your very best."*

In your career, you may occasionally daydream of "what ifs" and worry about things that are beyond your control. That's okay. It's natural for the mind to wander when faced with things like industry down cycles, personal slumps, and unforeseen roadblocks.

The cause for concern is when these negative thoughts consume one's mind, feeding fire to the stress of the situation, effectively preventing an individual from being at their *very best.*

Do you want to operate at your very best, even in the face of adversity? Spend time planning. Anticipate the elements or events that could slow your forward momentum. Worry about the controllables—the things that you can roll up your sleeves and fix. This mindset drives confidence, which creates a following. Your team members don't want just an "engaged manager," they want an "engaged leader," someone they can get behind, believe in, and support.

In challenging revenue years, you *need* everyone to be all-in and focused. Your team(s) understand this, and within reason, they'll anticipate you to turn up the heat a bit for increased performance.

"When we needed you the most, you gave us your very best." Hopefully, you've built a team about whom you can say this.

And, don't forget that simultaneously to you asking the question of your sellers, they are asking the very same question of you!

A PASSION FOR OUR INDUSTRY

My wife, Bridget, and I were spending a long overdue catch-up evening with lifelong friends, Rocky and Angie. They were high school sweethearts, and as of this writing, have been married for nearly 25 years. They're the kind of friends we never see often enough, but when we do, there's instant comfort, and the laughs come so freely it's as if no time has passed.

As the evening progressed, the memories began to flow. Rocky and I were convincing each other that we could still strap on a football helmet and compete with even the best high school football stars, while Angie and Bridget rolled their eyes, communicating a non-verbal "yeah, right."

The conversation had turned to "...I wonder what 'so and so' does now...," when Angie interjected, "John, I remember that in seventh grade you gave an oral report on how you wanted to be in broadcasting. You wanted to be a disc jockey."

Now, Angie and I have known each other since first grade. She could have recalled any memory, such as my bloody nose at recess, our moments with the wildest math teacher in the history of education, or even me taking her sister to prom. But, instead, her top of mind was that I had wanted to be in broadcasting. She went on to comment, "Everyone knew you were headed to broadcasting. You spoke so passionately about it."

Retrospectively, Angie was right. The many hours of playing make-believe DJ on my mom's portable turntable gave way to a real-life disc jockey job at radio station WIRO at the age of 15.

Between 15 and 18, news reporting, sports play-by-play, promotions, and production skills were all added to my résumé. Then, on high school graduation day, in a pre-college effort to move to the broadcasting "money," I accepted a promotion to station account executive.

Ultimately, my career tracks took me from radio to TV, seller to management, station management to corporate TV, and corporate TV to industry consultant, speaker, and author. Since that oral report in seventh grade, I've never looked back and have never regretted the decision to commit my career and life to an industry I love. It's often surprising, but also fulfilling, to run into so many people who have a similar history in broadcasting.

Why do I tell you this personal story? Because, in my opinion, this story, and so many like it, need to be told. As an industry, we have lost our enthusiasm for what got us to the dance, as hours turn into lost days of crunching numbers behind closed doors. So, now and again, a reminder of how and why one arrived (not to be confused with rearview mirror regrets) can do wonders for the mind when one of those less-than-enjoyable days surfaces.

The new faces you're hiring and mentoring in our business need to hear these stories. However, when telling your personal story, resist the urge to wax eloquently about the good ol' days. Instead, discuss career satisfaction, the voice of experience your mentors provided, what it means to be a professional in this business, and the responsibility and pride that accompanies representing a legacy.

Why am I in broadcasting? For me, it was, and still is, the fun, the positive impact for clients, and the ability to affect community change. In summary, it's a passion. Despite the bad days and the fear of industry change(s), the anticipation of good... no, great... days, and passion is what drove me to this incredible industry, and it's what still keeps me in it today!

What's your story?

THE FINAL LESSON

LIVE LIFE ENGAGED

As I write this, multi-screen coverage continues from Las Vegas, the site of the deadliest mass shooting in modern US history (59 dead, and 527 injured.) This heart-breaking news follows professional athletes kneeling in protest during the national anthem; hurricane devastation in Puerto Rico, Texas and Florida; North Korea's bombing threats; earthquake damage in Mexico; and race riots in Missouri and Virginia. There has been no shortage of unbelievable headlines the past couple of years. This period in our history is defined by societal division and suffering. It seems voices are getting louder and the defense of passionate beliefs is accompanied by combative tones.

Have you noticed any changes in the people around you? Have your dinner topics gravitated to the events at hand? It there a lack of laughter at the office water cooler? Are employees moving slower, spending more time reading headlines instead of making sales calls? Is there an air of concern or even anxiety in the hallways?

In 2001, I can remember how our television station employees were consumed with the incredible devastation of 9-11. No one in the station personally knew anyone who died or immediately suffered from this terrorist act. In fact, the station was over 2,100 miles away from ground zero. However, the incident was a human tragedy, and because we are human, all hearts were affected. I proposed the best course of action for our team members was to go sit with their clients, and simply listen.

To be fair, when presented with tragic news, individuals are affected differently. A few are truly not bothered. However, the majority will compartmentalize their feelings or maybe voice a brief concern or opinion to get a group temperature check. Then there are those who wear their feelings on their sleeves. You know exactly where they stand on the subject.

So, as a manager striving to be a leader, what can you do to help ease the anxiety of those around you?

Your job is to cast aside any barriers that would prohibit you from being approachable. Convey how important individuals are to you by making small gestures, such as turning away from your computer screen when someone enters your office, or removing physical separators by getting up and walking around a desk to take a seat next to an employee for a discussion. When approached in the hallway, pocket your mobile phone to stop the urge to multi-task.

Check in often and make yourself available for conversations. Offer opinions when asked, act as a moderator to allow a voice for opposing thoughts, and gently cool any heat that may arise from disagreements.

For optimal engagement, accelerate your MBWA (Management By Walking Around.) When doing so, look for opportunities to deliver heartfelt connections. Recognize when someone needs a hug (being mindful of their personal space), but also be prepared to offer honest feedback. Remind individuals how important they are to the team, to the clients and to their families, and strive to create an air of "we're in this together."

Have you considered actions to lighten any "heavy air" to help ease team tension? Play music at every opportunity you can find. It has been said that "music sooths the weary soul." It doesn't cost you anything to experiment to see if that statement holds true.

Bring in food, for no reason at all. Who doesn't smile when they discover the occasional surprise brownie?

Tell corny jokes and ask the team to share some of their favorites. Shared laughter is very therapeutic, memorable, and a great positive momentum team builder.

For your own sanity, get in a workout. Daily exercise slows an overwhelmed mind, dampens anxiety, and provides clarity in decision-making.

Find a cause to support and volunteer. Selfishly, helping others makes one's heart feel good, and as a bonus, helps the community.

Share open dialogue with family members and trusted friends. Hug them a little longer, tell them how fortunate you *feel* that they're in your life, and don't be afraid to pen a note of appreciation or connect with another, "I love you."

As I type these thoughts, it's apparent that *engagement* is extremely important during times of adversity. But how good of an engaged manager could you be if you practiced these steps on a day-to-day basis, regardless of environmental conditions? Think back on your career and life mentors. Those individuals saw something in you that you didn't see. They said, "You can" when you were saying, "I can't." They helped you understand the difference between right and wrong and how important it is to always do the right thing, especially when no one was looking.

If it hasn't occurred to you previously, the magic—the one thing that all of these positive influencers who exit and enter your life have in common—can be summarized in four short words—they live life *engaged*.

ABOUT THE AUTHOR

John Hannon is an in-demand keynote speaker and management and leadership thought leader. He works with television companies to develop profitable strategies for both media outlets and client advertisers. His extensive knowledge of television management, marketing, digital convergence, and sales enables him to help industry leaders create powerful selling cultures to dramatically grow their businesses.

His broadcasting career began at the age of fifteen as a radio station disc jockey. By the age of eighteen, John answered the call of customer service as an account executive.

He offers clients an impressive portfolio of experience, having held various sales, station management, program distribution, and corporate positions with Tri-Radio Broadcasting, ACT III, Sullivan Broadcasting, Sinclair Broadcasting, Quorum Broadcasting, and Acme Communications.

Under John's leadership, television stations have won five #1 in the nation awards, the network Model For Success, the Better Business Bureau Integrity Award, and multiple National Association of

Broadcasting Sales Promotion awards.

Most recently, John was President of Jim Doyle & Associates, a marketing firm of speakers, authors, trainers, and consultants dedicated to helping television sales organizations consistently deliver significant revenue increases. During his tenure, the company annually made over 5,000 sales calls and wrote over $50,000,000 in digital and television revenue for their partner stations.

John is an Amazon best-selling author, having achieved the #1 best-seller in the category of Management & Leadership: Training, and a #1 new release ranking. His *Engaged Management* book series consists of *Volume 1, Inspiring Your Team To Win; Volume 2, Maximizing Your Team's Sales Performance*; and *Volume 3, Engaged Management, Awakening Sales Confidence In Your Team.*

Originally from Ironton Ohio, John holds degrees from Central Texas College and Ohio University. He completed his Master's degree in Journalism and Broadcast Station Management at Marshall University. He is a member of the National Speakers Association and has achieved the Certified Speaking Professional (CSP) designation. Only 1.4% (761) of the over 53,000 speakers worldwide hold the CSP credential.

John is a nearly twelve-year veteran of the Air Force, Air Force Reserve, and Army National Guard.

He is a retired rugby player living in Sarasota, Florida, with wife Bridget, two daughters, a son, and two dogs.

CONTACTS

John M. Hannon
John Hannon Media, LLC
7762 Silver Bell Drive
Sarasota, FL 34241

937-776-4997
john@johnhannonmedia.com
www.johnhannonmedia.com

 /johnhannonmedia

 /in/johnhannonmedia

 @johnhannonmedia

 youtube.com/c/johnhannonmedia

Made in the
USA
Columbia, SC